100 YEARS

Other Works by George P. Berg

Letters Home: Reflections of a Marine Rifleman

Grunt 0311: Reflections of a Marine Rifleman

Managing Construction Changes: Calculating the Cost

Improving Construction Productivity: Case Studies for Success

100 YEARS

One Family's History in the United States Air Force

1917-2026

George P. Berg

100 Years: One Family's History in the United States Air Force, 1917-2026
Ben Wheeler, Texas
Copyright 2026 George P. Berg
ISBN 979-8-9952801-0-1
ISBN 979-8-9952801-1-8 (epub)

Dedicated to the Next Generation

Jacob Stouffer Barber
Grady Patrick Barber
Maclyn Lawrence Barber
Abigail Frances Berg
Adelyn Avery Berg
Brynley Ann Berg
Hannah Jane Berg
Bridger James Kilpatrick
Jones Michael Kilpatrick

Table of Contents

Section 5

Preface

OUR UNITED STATES AIR FORCE family started four generations ago in 1917. Through birth and marriage, the legacy of air service has continued for more than 100 years.

My grandfather served in the Army Air Service from 1917–1919. I stumbled upon his uniform while on summer vacation to the family farm in Illinois. He was a legend in our family and respected by everyone. I wanted to know more about him and why he was the way he was—a reserved gentleman.

It occurred to me that I didn't fully understand my own US Air Force father. Where did he come from? What was his childhood like and how did we ended up an Air Force family? Was I influenced by his service when I joined the US Marine Corps? I didn't know anything about my father's family's history of military service. Why was he so different than my mother's family?

Researching our family Air Force history, I also realized I had underestimated my younger brother Malcolm and his service in the US Air Force. I was proud of his scholastic and military accomplishments but only vaguely understood what it took for him to be as successful as he was in the Air Force and later as a civilian.

Malcolm's oldest son followed the oversized imprint made by his father. Stephen is a perfect match for his Air Force career path, almost as if it was preordained. His outstanding career is ongoing. There's a very good chance he will conclude his career as the highest-ranking officer in our family's long US Air Force history.

These pages only cover the first one hundred years of service to our country. The future may hold more.

SECTION 1

Chapter 1

Grandparents' Farm

SOMETIMES IN THE SUMMER, my family visited our grandparents' farm in Northern Illinois. It was a delight. We looked forward to this specific vacation with enthusiasm and joy. On the farm there were cattle, horses, chickens, cats, and dogs to fill our days. My oldest brother Steve and I ran in the tall cornfields and explored the old horse barn and corn crib. At the end of the mile-long fields, a deep drainage ditch had been dug decades before. We waded in the clear cool water, precariously balancing ourselves across the rickety beaver dams. We played outside the entire day.

At sundown, my father's distinctive recall whistle or our grandmother's call, "Boys," summoned us for dinner. Occasionally after eating, we went back outside to catch fireflies and put them in a glass jar. We set the flashing bugs on our nightstand and watched them glow until we fell asleep.

The farmhouse was a two-story, wood frame with white shiplap siding. A partially enclosed sunporch was attached in the front. The house had a large living room with a comfortable couch and overstuffed chairs. But the kitchen was where we spent much of our time, if we were indoors.

When my brothers and I came down for breakfast in the morning, Grama quarantined on the steps in the narrow hallway leading to the bedrooms. We could only watch from that vantage point in anticipation as our grandmother rolled out the soon-to-be-frosted cinnamon rolls. When they were done baking, the pleasant aroma of cinnamon filled the entire house. Before we were allowed to taste a single morsel, we had to finish our hearty breakfast of farm-fresh eggs and bacon.

Upstairs there were three bedrooms and a room used for storage; it was off limits, restricted access only. Grama constantly reminded us, "Boys, do not go in this room. We don't want you messing around in there. Do you understand?"

We replied in unison, "Yes, Grama."

Then she looked down her nose at me. "George, especially you, George. Do you promise?"

I nodded that I did.

But I was curious about the room. One day while everyone else was occupied, I peaked in. I saw nothing special: an old pedal-powered sewing machine, a banjo, clothes folded in an old fashioned wooden and leather steamer trunk, yellowing photographs hanging on the wall—many of south Texas— and other odds and ends. A neatly coiled lariat with a leather-reinforced Hondo was draped on a closet hook. I found out later it was an authentic cactus fiber lasso purchased just over the Texas border in Mexico.

On a sturdy wooden coat hanger in a corner was a gray wool military uniform. I was familiar with uniforms; our dad was in the US Air Force, but I had never seen one like this. It had a high collar and burnished pewter-colored buttons. The uniform looked stiff and formal.

Over the left-hand pocket was the most handsome set of wings I had ever seen. The badge had a shield of stars and stripes with the capital letters US in the middle. Shining metallic eagle feathers reached out from the center of the shield. I stared at it, fascinated.

1.1. World War I pilots wings like those awarded to Second Lieutenant Herbert N Parker.

I smiled, satisfied with my risky adventure into the unknown. I stood looking around at all the musky history saved in that room. History we knew nothing about. Suddenly, I saw a shadow on the wall. It was cast over me and getting bigger.

"George, you are in trouble! You are not supposed to be in here, are you? Did you touch anything?"

"No, Grama, nothing."

To salve her disappointment and distract her, I asked, "What's that gray uniform over there? Whose was that?"

She said, "It was your grandfather's uniform in World War One. He was a pilot."

My imagination took flight. How could our gentle, old farmer—our grampa—have been a pilot and fight in a war?

Over the next few years, we learned more from townspeople and distant relatives. People told me Grampa was a fighter pilot that had faced German pilots and shot them down. He was a member of the famous Escadrille, made up of American pilots who volunteered to fly in France. Before the American Army Air Service, he enlisted in the Canadian Army so he could join the fight in Europe with other members of the Phi Delta Theta Canadian fraternities. He attended the University of Wisconsin and pledged to the Phi Delta Theta fraternity when he was only fifteen years old. How many of those fables and tall tales were true? I spent hours wondering about them. He was my hero.

Herbert Parker was a tall, striking man with long gray hair, kept neatly combed and parted. His face was handsome but stern, with seldom a smile. I don't remember hearing him ever laugh aloud. He was stoic. His cheeks and chin were clean shaven, but he sported a neatly trimmed mustache. Even in his old age, he walked straight up, shoulders back, taking confident, measured steps.

As a farmer, he had strong callused hands and scarlet cheeks weathered permanently by the sun. His forehead, however, was pale and white; it was shielded from exposure to the elements by his wide-brimmed cap he always wore while outside.

He wore a black eyepatch pirate-style over the place where the left eye he lost in a serious farming accident had been. The eyeglasses he wore to read had an opaque coating on the inside of the lens that covered his missing eye.

His injury didn't interfere with working every day on the farm. Usually, he was on his John Deere tractor, plowing or cultivating rows of oats, soybeans, or corn. He kept a steady pace, working until dark most days. He earned the respect everyone gave him.

In the evenings, a washbowl, soap, and towel waited in the entryway where he cleaned up. Herbert would take off his laced leather boots, leaving them by the door for the next morning's work. Then he climbed the steep stairs to change his clothes for dinner.

He didn't talk much but always thanked our grandmother for the evening meal, then slowly pushed himself away from the table. Tired, he went to the screened-in porch to read. Like clockwork, Grandma or our mom took him a bowl of buttered popcorn, slices of cheddar cheese, and half an apple with the core removed. He read by a small lamp—a book, the *National Geographic Magazine*, or occasionally the Sears, Roebuck catalog.

I would sit next to him but not too close. My mom brought me a salad bowl of popcorn and a ten-year-old boy's proportions of cheese and apple. My favorite reading material (thumbing through the photographs) was the latest *National Geographic*, particularly when the articles were about Africa. The semi-naked, topless tribeswomen fascinated me. I was spellbound. That was until I heard my grandfather say, "Turn the page, George."

Begrudgingly, I slowly turned the page. He knew our wild nature and tolerated us being boys. He had two sons, George and Gordon. He was familiar with raucous young men. His oldest child was our mother, Caroline. She had three sons, so there were always curious and occasionally mischievous boys around.

Grampa was my hero when I was ten. I didn't truly understand what a hero he was until I grew up and looked into his military history.

Chapter 2

Herbert Nichols Parker

EFFIE NICHOLS PARKER WAS born in Delavan on May 5, 1867. Her husband Edwin Parker was two years older, born in 1865, also in Delavan. Both were from prominent families.

Edwin was the second son of the beloved town doctor. Effie was a Nichols (a wealthy family). They must have known each other from primary school through high school.

Traditional for the times, Effie was a homemaker. Because Edwin had various occupations—chief among them accounting—the family traveled here and there.

The only child of Edwin and Effie, Herbert N. Parker was born on the Fourth of July in 1895, in Delavan, Illinois. At the time, Delavan was a town of about 1,750 people, located in the middle of Illinois, thirty miles south of Peoria. The town was founded by a group of settlers from Rhode Island and derives its name from Edward C. Delavan, a temperance advocate from Albany, New York. The early village of Delavan was conservative by design. The post office has been in operation since 1840.

Edwin had a wanderlust and moved the family frequently, but Herbert stayed close to his maternal grandfather EF, who provided stability and consistency. EF was Herbert's rock.

GRANDFATHER EDWAN FRANKLIN NICHOLS (EF)

EF was from New Hampshire by way of New York but decided to uproot the family and head to the new frontier: Illinois and the west. They settled in Delavan, Illinois. At the time, inexpensive, fertile farmland was becoming available. One of the intriguing places for settlers was in Northern Illinois near the villages surrounding the town of Dixon: Ashton, West Brooklyn, Amboy. and Lee Center, all about 125 miles north of Delavan. The area contained vast marshlands primarily in Lee County. The local name of the vast undeveloped area was simply "The Swamp."

EF Nichols purchased large portions of the land around the soggy bog that, at the time, appeared relatively worthless. His observation of similar properties around Delavan, Illinois, prompted him to buy and develop swampland in northern Illinois. In so doing, he created a fortune for himself and future generations.

EF's ingenuity and vision allowed Herbert to have a life of privilege. Because of him, Herbert became a member of the landed gentry, status few others enjoyed at that time.

2.1. Herbert, Edwin and Effie Parker (circa 1900)

Chapter 3

Herbert's Schooling

HERBERT NICHOLS PARKER'S EDUCATION was interrupted by his father's different employments. One of Herbert's report cards showed better than average grades, his family's transient nature notwithstanding. He attended high school in Indiana; Rockford, Illinois; and finally graduated from The Wisconsin High School of the University of Wisconsin in 1916. High school graduation rates were only about 14 percent.

THE WISCONSIN HIGH SCHOOL

OF

THE UNIVERSITY OF WISCONSIN

Fifth Annual Commencement

SATURDAY EVENING, JUNE 10, 1916

AT

EIGHT O'CLOCK

ASSEMBLY ROOM
WISCONSIN HIGH SCHOOL

3.1. Wisconsin high school graduation, 1916

On July 21, 1916, he began at the University of Wisconsin's College of Liberal Arts and Sciences. At the time, only 3-4 percent of men graduated from college, and fewer women. Most of the population was engaged in agriculture one way or another. Formal education was not seen as important, except for the aristocratic scions of elite families.

Herbert, thanks to his grandfather EF, was one of them.

At the time, the University of Wisconsin (UW) was recognized as a distinguished college by the war department. It played a significant role in preparing students for military service, especially during World War I. The university offered intensive military training courses and had an officer training corps on camps in full operation even before the Preparedness Movement and the establishment of the official reserve officer training corps program in 1916.

Many university departments offered classes specifically designed to prepare students for various wartime roles, including telegraphers, wireless operators, aviation, engineers, and more. Students could even earn academic credit for participating in military service or related training with credits being awarded for actual service as well as coursework.

Herbert wanted to fly, so he requested to be trained as a soldier at Plattsburg, New York, as part of the burgeoning Preparedness Movement.

In August 1916, the roster of enrollees showed that Herbert was at the Federal Military Training Camp in Plattsburg. He spent most of the remaining summer there learning how to be a soldier, marching in formation, and horseback riding. The cadets were taught military courtesy and commands, the use of weapons, and tactics and strategy.

PLATTSBURG

PLATTSBURG WAS AN IDEAL spot for a civilian training camp for college students like Herbert. Later, older wealthy businessmen were also invited to receive military training, to be ready to fight in case the United States was invaded.

Plattsburg is 150 miles north of Albany, New York, and accessible via rail and auto, with ferries running daily from Burlington and other points on Lake Champlain. Water was plentiful, and the surrounding countryside was sparsely settled. The town was modern enough, carried metropolitan newspapers, and boasted adequate tourist accommodation, including the beautiful hotel Champlain situated on a bluff overlooking the lake, perhaps the finest hotel in all northern New York.

Rolling terrain and numerous streams provided variety for military maneuvers. The fact that the garrison was essentially a training post complete with rifle range and parade ground made it adaptable to a large influx of rookie recruits—future citizen soldiers. Albany Road ran through the middle of the camp and to the west was the mile long parade ground.

The camp was bounded on three sides by tall groves of oak and maple. To the east, the part of Lake Champlain known as Cumberland Bay was studded with small islands of pine and rock. Patches of poison ivy notwithstanding, the lakeshore became a haven in late afternoons as bone-sore, perspiring recruits tried to splash a little feeling back into their bodies before the bugler signaled retreat.

Herbert, like most young men, was changed by his experience at Plattsburg over the summer of 1916. He was even more enamored by the thought of being in the military. More than ever, he wanted to fly airplanes.

When he returned to enjoy the fall semester at UW, he interviewed for a popular fraternity and was accepted. Herbert Nichols Parker was initiated into the Phi Delta Theta fraternity on April 28, 1917. His bond number was 422. The Phi Delts, as they are referred to, was an international fraternity with houses in Toronto and Montreal, Canada.

Chapter 4

Registering for the Draft

THE WAR HAD BEEN ongoing in Europe since 1914. Canada, as part of the Commonwealth of the British Empire, was committed to fight.

The United States was not at war, but on June 5, 1917, Herb Parker was required to register for the military draft in Dixon, Illinois. He indicated his occupation was "farmhand" employed by Gustav Haushaar. His registration card also said he was a private in the infantry with the Cadet Corps at the University of Wisconsin.

On that same day, millions of men, ages twenty-one to forty-five, appeared before local boards to provide information to determine their suitability for potential military service. Local authorities determined whether a man would be drafted or if they rated an exemption for having a critical war-related job or being the sole provider for children.

The previous experience of conscription in the United States during the Civil War led to claims of inequality when wealthy draftees could pay their way out of service while poor draftees could not. In New York City during the Civil War, riots erupted over the issuance of forced military service.

The World War I system—termed Selective Service—had better results. There was minor draft resistance, and the system still had loopholes (African Americans were proportionately more likely to be selected for service than their White counterparts). Still, by the end of the war, 2.8 million men were successfully drafted into the military out of roughly 4.6 million total service members.

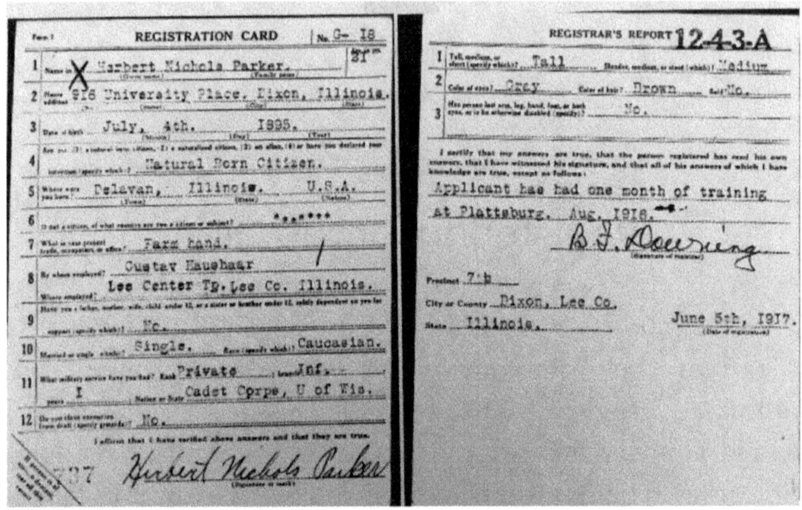

4.1. Herbert Parker draft registration card, 1917

CANADIAN ARMY SERVICE

Amongst the family, there has been discussion about Herbert serving in the Canadian Army.

I found a Canadian Over-Seas Expeditionary Force Attestation paper signed in 1915 with an identical name, similar signature, and same birthdate.

The possibility that Herbert served in the Canadian Army infantry is remote. He was in high school in 1915 in the United States. The American Herbert Parker probably did not serve in the Canadian Army. If by some fluke he did, he was certainly not deployed to Europe.

ORIGINAL

ATTESTATION PAPER
26TH OVERSEAS BATTALION
CANADIAN OVER-SEAS EXPEDITIONARY FORCE.

No. 775153

Folio.

QUESTIONS TO BE PUT BEFORE ATTESTATION.

(ANSWERS).

1. What is your surname? .... Parker
1a. What are your Christian names? .... Herbert
1b. What is your present address? .... 282 Evelyn Ave., Toronto.
2. In what Town, Township or Parish, and in what Country were you born? .... West Toronto
3. What is the name of your next-of-kin? .... Mr. George H. Parker
4. What is the address of your next-of-kin? .... 282 Evelyn Ave., Toronto
4a. What is the relationship of your next-of-kin? .... Father
5. What is the date of your birth? .... Jan'y 4, 1895
6. What is your Trade or Calling? .... Driver
7. Are you married? .... No
8. Are you willing to be vaccinated or re-vaccinated and inoculated? .... Yes
9. Do you now belong to the Active Militia? .... No
10. Have you ever served in any Military Force? .... No
    If so, state particulars of former service.
11. Do you understand the nature and terms of your engagement? .... Yes
12. Are you willing to be attested to serve in the CANADIAN OVER-SEAS EXPEDITIONARY FORCE? .... Yes

DECLARATION TO BE MADE BY MAN ON ATTESTATION.

I, ... Herbert Parker ...., do solemnly declare that the above are answers made by me to the above questions and that they are true, and that I am willing to fulfil the engagements by me now made, and I hereby engage and agree to serve in the Canadian Over-Seas Expeditionary Force, and to be attached to any arm of the service therein, for the term of one year, or during the war now existing between Great Britain and Germany should that war last longer than one year, and for six months after the termination of that war provided His Majesty should so long require my services, or until legally discharged.

Herbert Parker (Signature of Recruit)

Date ....December 28th 1915   *W. G. McKay* (Signature of Witness)

OATH TO BE TAKEN BY MAN ON ATTESTATION.

I, ... Herbert Parker ...., do make Oath, that I will be faithful and bear true Allegiance to His Majesty **King George the Fifth**, His Heirs and Successors, and that I will as in duty bound honestly and faithfully defend His Majesty, His Heirs and Successors, in Person, Crown and Dignity, against all enemies, and will observe and obey all orders of His Majesty, His Heirs and Successors, and of all the Generals and Officers set over me. So help me God.

Herbert Parker (Signature of Recruit)

Date .... December 28th 1915 .... *W. G. McKay* (Signature of Witness)

CERTIFICATE OF MAGISTRATE.

The Recruit above-named was cautioned by me that if he made any false answer to any of the above questions he would be liable to be punished as provided in the Army Act.
The above questions were then read to the Recruit in my presence.

4.2. Canadian Attestation for Herbert H Parker, December 28, 1915

WORLD WAR I

The war Herbert volunteered to be in was one of deadliest conflicts in history. It resulted in the estimated 30 million military casualties and another 8 million civilian deaths from war-related causes, disease, and genocide.

In the meantime, Herbert's interest in aviation wasn't lessened by the primitive design and flimsy materials of the aircraft. Only fourteen years had passed since the Wright brothers made their first flights near Kitty Hawk. The war brought about major acceleration in the development of everything about aircraft, but they were still made if canvas and wood, held together by metal pipes and bailing wire.

Charles B. Flood, in his book *First to Fly*, quotes an Escadrille pilot.

> With only slight exaggeration, it seemed as if they were merely gathered up odds and ends of wood, discarded matchsticks and the like, which were wired together, catch-as catch-can fashion…Then old handkerchiefs were sewed together to cover the wings and that part of the fuselage around the pilot seat. The remainder of the fuselage was left naked which gave the plane a sort of half-finished appearance.

The war being fought in Europe had raged for three long years before the US entered the fighting. Soon Herbert would join the war.

After registering for the draft in Dixon in June 1917, Herbert returned to Madison. There he said goodbye to his fraternity brothers and took care of his affairs. It is unknown exactly how many of his brothers also resigned from the fraternity to fight in the war, but many of them did.

His occupation as a farmhand on his draft card could have earned him a deferment, but Herb felt it was his duty as an aristocratic upper-class gentleman to enlist in the Army. Instead of waiting for induction, he joined the Army, requesting to be in the newly formed branch of the Signal Corps—the Army Air Service.

Air Service was reserved for the best and brightest, college-educated, and the fool hearty. Because of his studies at the university, Herb was selected. Private Parker reported to Chicago, Illinois, for his pre-aviation examination. He passed the physical and mental requirements and was accepted as a candidate for the Air Service.

Chapter 5

Military Service

AUSTIN, TEXAS

A LONG WITH HUNDREDS of other young men, Herbert Parker joined the aviation ground school on October 14, 1917, at the University of Texas in Austin.

When Herb arrived, only a few buildings and part of a field existed. The new airfield was established for the School of Military Avionics conducted by the University of Texas for the United States government. The Army Signal Corps deemed the area suitable for a landing field and approved the site.

According to the USAF Historical Division, Air University, the initial training was discretionary, and college professors followed a suggested syllabus. Later, the training course of study became standardized; the curriculum borrowed from the Canadians.

ORDERED TO SIGNAL CORPS

Herbert N. Parker Told To Report To Austin, Texas.

Herbert N. Parker, the 21 year old son of Mr. and Mrs. E. W. Parker of 916 University Place, has been asked to report at once to Austin, Tex.

On Sept. 1st the young man passed the examination for the aviation branch of the signal corps. Just now he is visiting his grandfather in Delavan, Ill.

5.1. Herbert Parker to Report to Signal Corps (used with permission from Newspapers.com)

It included understanding engines, observation, meteorology, signaling, gunnery, and bombing from airplanes. There was a total of 133 hours. Strict military discipline was enforced. The training subsequently included navigation.

5.2. Private Herbert Parker, Aviation Ground School, Austin, Texas, 1917

Flying in the military was still in its infancy. The idea of being one of the first airmen to volunteer to go to war in airplanes was a testament to Herbert's courage as well that of his classmates. The ground school training in Austin lasted three months.

In January of 1918, Private Parker reported to his flight training squadron at Ellington Field, near Houston, Texas. Ellington Field was under construction at the time, so conditions were as sparse as they were in Austin.

Ellington Field

In November of 1917, the 120th Aero Squadron was transferred from Kelly Field near San Antonio to Ellington Field in Houston, Texas. Much of the construction of the base was finished by December, but Ellington Field had a chronic shortage of trained personnel, with only 120 men stationed at the airfield. Personnel problems were so grave, the war department allowed officials at Ellington to use the direct enlistment of men to fill the ranks, allowing local men to enlist in the Army, reporting directly to Ellington Field.

Only a few US Army Air Service aircraft arrived with the squadrons, mostly the Curtiss JN "Jennies." The planes were shipped in wooden crates by railcar.

5.3. Curtiss JN Ellington Field, Houston Texas, 1918 (aeropedia photo)

In December 1917, the first planes from Ellington field flew over Houston. A flight of ten JN-4s took off from the grass fields and followed the interurban tracks stretching from Genoa to Houston.

Because of the lack of military pilots, the US Army Air Service relied on civilian and British pilots to help train cadets. Civilian pilots often had more flight experience than military aviators. Upon graduation, a flight cadet was christened as a military aviator.

In 1918, Herbert's flight training occurred in two phases: primary and advanced.

Primary training took eight weeks and consisted of pilots learning basic flying skills using both dual and solo instruction, including practice on bombing and gunnery ranges located on a small peninsula jutting into the Gulf of Mexico near San Leon, Texas.

ANOTHER DIXON BOY WRITES OF EXPERIENCES

'ABOARD U. S. AIRPLANE 2,000 FEET IN THE AIR

We are allowed to quote from a letter from Herbert N. Parker, who is at the Ellington Field near Houston, Tex., in the aviation service, written to his mother, Mrs. E. W. Parker:

"We are here for at least three months and since the government issues us only a limited amount of equipment, I'll have to have a few more things to make me more comfortable while here. I don't expect to get to town from now on and won't take any chance to go, as I am more than interested in the flying game and will stay right on the job and learn as much of it as I can instead of running into town. I have flown and handled the controllers in the air, but haven't taken a 'ship' up alone yet, probably will be doing such work within a couple of weeks at least. I suppose you are interested to know how I felt on my first flight. Experienced no unusual sensation and had no feeling of fear or feeling such as one has in a rapidly descending elevator. The ground simply leaves you and objects on it become smaller and smaller as you go up. There is much noise from the engine and a great rush of air.

"It is quite the most wonderful thing I ever experienced and I am crazy to go up all the time. The speed doesn't seem great when you are flying 2,000 feet altitude. One seems to float along. My ears tingle and there is a roaring sound in them from the rapid change of altitude, although I did my flying this morning, and it is now bedtime. I have applied for $10,000 of insurance and made it payable to you. I have gotten interested in reading again and grab every chance I get to read. I have been reading Kipling and Pickwick papers and have enjoyed them very much, which shows that I am not as nervous as I was at Austin (Ground School), because I could not sit down and read there.

"Later. Have just returned from a nice flying trip. Saw the first accident this afternoon. A cadet fell about 3,000 feet in a trial speed; of course he was killed. He probably fainted or got scared. This is the first accident that has happened at this field so far. They are no more common than automobile accidents are, so you don't need to waste any time worrying. The weather has moderated some and it is much more comfortable. This will have to be all for this time, because a fellow cadet has lit on my bunk in preparation for a talk fest."

5.4. Dixon Evening Telegraph. Letter from Herbert, Ellington Field, Houston, Texas, 1918

Promoted to second lieutenant, Herbert Parker got his pilot's wings at Ellington Field in Houston, Texas, in 1918, flying Curtiss JN-4s. Herbert was then transferred to Fort Sill, Oklahoma, for advanced training.

5.5. Herbert N Parker flight trainee, Texas, 1918

FORT SILL

Fort Sill was the first home of Army aviation with the First Aerial Squadron on July 26, 1915, when eight Curtiss JN-3 airplanes arrived from Rockwell Field, California. The squadron was ordered to Fort Sill because of a raid by Villa which threatened war between United States and Mexico. The aviation field facilities at Fort Sill were just a little more than grass fields used as a base of operations.

5.6. Curtiss JN Fort Sill, Oklahoma, 1917 (US Army Museum, Fort Sill, public domain)

In 1918 at advanced training, Herbert learned flying techniques that made him a more proficient pilot. It consisted of six intense weeks of cockpit flight and classroom instruction. Herb Parker trained to be a bomber pilot and an aerial gunner.

From Oklahoma, Herbert transferred to Camp Taliaferro near Fort Worth, Texas.

TO LEARN AERIAL GUNNERY

Lt. Herbert N. Parker of the Aviation Section, Signal Officers Reserve Corps, who has been flying at Ft. Sill, Okla., has been transferred to Taliaferro field near Ft. Worth, Texas, for practice in aerial gunnery.

5.6. Dixon evening Telegraph, 1918 (used with permission)

CAMP TALIAFERRO, TEXAS

Early in 1918 Herbert moved to Camp Taliaferro for observation and advanced aerial gunnery. The warmer weather in Texas was more conducive for flight training year-round.

Pilots were trained on the Curtiss JN-4 biplane. Jennies had a maximum speed of about seventy-five miles an hour. Some Jennies had machine guns and bomb racks mounted for advanced training, but most did not. The JN series featured a combination of the best attributes of Curtiss J and the N models.

Herb trained in 1918 but in the years before the JN-3 version was the plane that supported Pershing's punitive expedition in Mexico to find Poncho Villa—the "infamous Mexican bandit" in 1915.

But by 1916, the aircraft proved unsuitable for field operations. At a top speed of 75 mph, it was an easy target for small arms fire, and there were issues with vulnerability, performance, and logistics.

The US improved the JN and redesigned it as the JN 4. With America's entry in the war on April 6, 1917, the Signal Corps ordered large quantities of NJ-4s for use as training aircraft.

When Herb relocated to Fort Worth in 1918, some of the specialized training was conducted by the British who had combat experience.

Aerial gunnery involved shooting at a moving target from a moving aircraft. Trainees started out with BB or pellets guns to learn how to lead a moving target. An expression heard often was "shoot them in the face." In other words, shoot at least one aircraft-length in front of the enemy, adjusting for the air speed of both planes.

Shot guns and skeet shooting were part of the curriculum until the cadet was proficient and graduated to larger static and then moving targets from a mock cockpit or back seat.

5.7. British sergeant provides instruction for a Lewis gun, June 1918 (N.A.R.A. photograph)

5.8. Using a wooden mockup of a Lewis Gun simulating rocking and jerking (N.A.R.A. photograph)

FRANCE

So far, Herbert had relocated from Dixon and Chicago, Illinois to Madison, Wisconsin; traveled to Austin Texas; down to Houston; then to Oklahoma; to Fort Worth; and finally back to Houston. He was awarded his pilot's wings and trained in aerial gunnery. He was ready to go to the war in Europe.

On August 22, 1918, Second Lieutenant Parker boarded a former Dutch passenger liner that was requisitioned by the Navy as a transport ship. He traveled from Hoboken, New Jersey to France. Between September and October 1918, Herbert remained near Brest, on the coast of France.

Once he completed in-processing, there was a period when newly arrived troops waited to limit the spread of influenza deemed inaccurately the "Spanish Flu." The pandemic was ravaging Europe, especially on the battlefields. In a letter home, Second Lieutenant Parker mentioned his time at Brest before shipping out to his next duty station.

FROM LIEUT. PARKER.

Under date of Sept. 9th, Herbert N. Parker, second lieutenant in the Air Service, Casual, A. P. O. 725, A E. F., writes his parents, Mr. and Mrs. E. W. Parker, from France:

Dear Folks:

The voyage over was without much excitement although submarines were seen several times. I'm now in the old town of Brest. It's a quaint old place with plenty of interest for the newcomer. The people are largely of the peasant class. This is the town where DeArtagnan, of the "Three Musketeers" started his adventure. It is a walled town and outside of the wall is a deep moat. Our camp is just outside of the city close to the moat. We can see down into the town from our position on a hill.

Just now there is an epidemic of influenza so we are forbidden to go into cafes, etc.

It rains every day and all day today, but it makes little difference in our daily program, which is doing

I have the French money system down pretty pat and know enough to order a meal or make a purchase. A few months over here ought to give anybody a working knowledge of French.

They serve wine in the officers' mess here at camp for 60c a bottle. It's very light stuff and tastes like weak vinegar.

I'm going down to a camp near ———— in a few days ————. I'm feeling all right so don't worry about me and be sure and take good care of yourselves.

Love to both.

HERB.

On October 2, 1918, Second Lieutenant Parker reported to the 7th Aviation Instruction Center (AIC) near Clermont-Ferrand, France, for bomber instruction. The Air Service mandated that all pilots go through a program of more advanced training, recognizing that the American pilots were not ready for the realities of actual aerial combat. The orientation included retraining in navigation, gunnery, engine

5.9. Dixon Telegraph, Oct 8, 1918 (used with permission)

maintenance, and repairs. From October through November, Herbert continued training.

Clermont is in the beautiful French countryside, surrounded by pastoral hills and bucolic but damp pastures. The base was established to train aviators in bombardment and bomber formation flying. The center was located near Michelin Air Testing Field and factory. The American Air Service relied exclusively on French planes and equipment. Pilots practiced both day and night bombing.

In the spring, around the time Herbert reported to the 7 AIC, the Air Service began receiving de Havilland DH-4s, an American-built bomber aircraft.

5.10. American built DeHavilland DH-4 (US Army Museum Fort Sill, Oklahoma, public domain)

The Air Service used DH-4s primarily for daytime bombing, observation, and artillery spotting. The first American DH-4 arrived in France in May 1918. The 138th Aerial Squadron flew the first DH for combat missions in early August of that year. DH-4 proved to be a huge success, considered the best single-engine bomber of WWI. Even when fully loaded with bombs, its reliability was maintained. DH-4's impressive performance proved highly popular with its crews, especially when fitted with Rolls Royce eagle engine. Its speed and altitude performance gave it a good deal of invulnerability to German fighter interceptors.

Unfortunately, the DH-4 had a few drawbacks, including its fuel system. The pressurized gas tank tended to explode. Also, its rubber fuel lines under the exhaust manifold caused fires. These problems led to the nickname "flaming coffin" even though only eight of the thirty-three DHs were lost in combat. In addition, the location of the gas tank between the pilot and observer limited communication. (National Museum of the United States Air Force).

While Second Lieutenant Parker was honing his flying skills in the new de Havilland, progress along the front lines continued. Germany's homefront and bankrupt government woes escalated. In October the German government pursued an end of the fighting. The Armistice was later signed and fighting stopped on November 11, 1918. The war officially ended on the eleventh hour on the eleventh day of the eleventh month. November 11 became American's Veterans' Day.

Second Lieutenant Parker continued training in Clermont while a program was developed for the demobilization for those soldiers not needed for occupation duty. Bomber pilots were not necessary for the occupation. Herbert's war was over.

HOMEWARD BOUND

Herbert staged to board a ship to the United States on January 8, 1919. The SS *Adriatic* set sail from Brest, France, for New Jersey on February 1, 1919. Herbert traveled to Garden City, where he was honorably discharged from the Army Air Service on February 6, 1919. Herbert accomplished his dream of being a military aviator. Throughout his military experience, he retained an attachment to Texas where he came of age as an airman.

STITZEL-PARKER—

Mr. and Mrs. George B. Stitzel, of 820 East Second street, announce the marriage of their daughter, Joy Marie, to Mr. Herbert N. Parker, son of Mr. and Mrs. E. W. Parker, of the Dixon Inn, as taking place at 4:30 Saturday afternoon, May 15, in Rockford. Rev. H. M. Bannen performed the ceremony at his residence. The young couple were unattended.

The bride wore a blue traveling suit with a hat to match. Her flowers were roses, arranged in a corsage bouquet.

The honeymoon will be spent in Wisconsin where they went by automobile after the ceremony.

Their residence will be divided between Dixon and Wisconsin, where Mr. Parker has farm interests.

The bride is a most attractive and vivacious young women. She is a graduate of the Dixon High school and since her graduation has been studying music. Mr. Parker was a Madison University student when the war broke out and he entered the aviation crops, going to France. He won a lieutenancy in the service. Both are very popular in the younger social set.

5.11. Wedding announcement for Herbert Parker and Joy Stitzel (Dixon Evening Telegraph, used with permission)

After being honorably discharged from the Army Air Service, Herbert returned to Dixon where he met Joy Stitzel, also from Dixon.

Joy's grandparents were from the Dakotas by way of Germany, as were almost 40 percent of immigrants at the time.

The wedding was in Rockford, forty miles from Dixon, and there were no guests. Apparently, the wedding was simple and brief. Perhaps the wedding was spartan because of the residual resentment of Germans. Parker is an English surname, and Stitzel is German. It's hard to imagine that Herbert and Joy were "both very popular with the younger social set," as stated in the newspaper of the time.

Frederick Luebke, in *Bonds of Loyalty: German American and World War I*, said, "In the anti-German hysteria of World War I, the assimilation of German-American was accelerated. And being a hyphenated American would mean being suspect in nativist eyes for decades to come."

As soon as the wedding was over, the new couple traveled to Wisconsin where the Parkers had property and business interests—onion farming.

Herbert Parker and Joy Stitzel had three children: Caroline, George, and Gordon. Both sons served in the military in WWII, George in the Army Air Corps and Gordon in the US Navy. Caroline, the oldest daughter, met Private Charles Berg, her future husband, in Chicago, Illinois, where he was on furlough while training for recruiting duty.

Caroline was a clothing and fabric buyer working for Killian department store on her lunch break.

SECTION 2

Charles Henry Berg Jr

CHARLES HENRY BERG JUNIOR was born on January 27, 1918, in Jacksonville, Florida. His parents were Charles Henry Senior and Georgia Virginia Tyler.

6.1. Georgia Virginia Tyler Berg, circa 1930s

Georgia had all the grace and manners of a southern lady with a silky gentile charm.

Charles Sr. was a hard-working linotype setter but gruff with a short temper. His driver's license for 1946 indicated his occupation as "Elec." (electrician).

6.2. Charles H. Berg Sr. Jacksonville Florida, circa 1920s

STATE OF FLORIDA DRIVER'S LICENSE

OPERATOR 1946	NOT GOOD AFTER OCTOBER 1, 1946
LICENSE No. 306730	CONDITIONS

DATE OF BIRTH	RACE	COLOR EYES	HEIGHT	WEIGHT
MO. 11 DAY 27 YEAR 84	W	brn	5 FT. 6 IN.	112 LBS.

DATE OF ISSUANCE	SEX	COLOR HAIR	OCCUPATION
MO. 9 DAY 5 YEAR 45	m	brn	Elec.

PRINT OR TYPE NAME: Charles Henry Berg
FIRST — MIDDLE OR MAIDEN — LAST

STREET AND NUMBER: 1404 Flagler Ave

CITY OR POSTOFFICE: Jax   Duval   Fla
COUNTY — STATE

I certify that my license is not under suspension or revocation in any state. (Signature) *Charles Henry Berg*

6.3. Charles H. Berg, Sr Drivers's License, 1946

6.4. Charles Sr. mixing a concoction on the bow of their boat, St. Johns River, Jacksonville, Florida, circa 1930s

As a young boy, Charles Jr. played outdoors like most children and enjoyed exploring the banks of the St. Johns River near his home. His family had a boat and a cabin on the river.

6.5. Charles Sr. hold Charles Jr. In the background, the building of the cabin on the St Johns River, 1920

6.6. Charles Sr. and Charles Jr., circa 1925

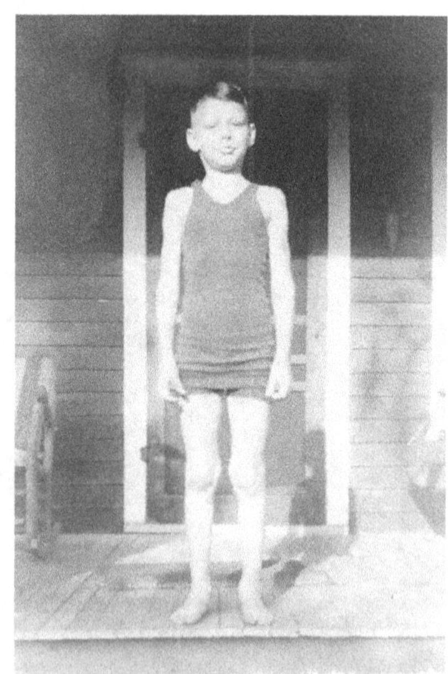

6.7. Charles Jr. at the cabin on the St Johns River, Florida, circa 1928

I suspect that Charles Sr was tough, hard-drinking, and rough on his only child Charles Jr.

Naturally inquisitive, he spent hours by himself reading about the natural world. Charles Jr. loved his youth in Florida (Spanish for "land of flowers"). He learned about the early myths and legends of the early native American and Spanish cultures.

When he became a father, he entertained me and my brothers with these tall tales. We thought his stories of the Florida swamps were unbelievable. As kids unfamiliar with that part of the south, they seemed outrageous; however, we found out later that many of them were true.

When Charles Jr. was young, he roamed in and explored the woods. He fished in the vast waterways, river systems, and ocean that surrounded early Jacksonville, Florida. Charles Jr. carved wooden knives and arrowheads. He made bows and arrows, complete with fletching made of feathers.

Charles Jr. attended public schools and graduated from high school in Jacksonville in 1937. During and after high school, Charles had a variety of jobs. He was a stevedore, unloading ships from central and south America.

But one of his favorite jobs was working as an usher and projectionist in the local movie house. He memorized the voices and script lines of famous characters and learned to imitate the accents of British actors.

In 1937-38, before Charles Jr. showed the feature film, there was a newsreel of national or international interest. Through newsreels, he kept well informed and acutely aware of world events. He shared as much of it as he could with us, teaching us the importance of world events from a very young age.

MILITARY SERVICE

In 1940, at the age of twenty-two, Charles Jr. joined Florida's Army National Guard and was assigned a military occupational specialty as a clerk-typist. His medical examination on February 24, 1940, at Fort McPhearson, Georgia, indicated nasopharyngitis (sinus infection) that was moderately severe. A similar condition was reported at the Station Hospital, Lowry Field, Denver, Colorado, on March 25, 1943. His sinus infections and the accompanying discomfort were chronic.

Private Charles Berg Jr. transferred to the regular Army infantry on October 9, 1940. He went on active duty January 6, 1941, when the unit was called to federal service under President Franklin D. Roosevelt's initiatives.

America entered World War II (WWII) on December 7, 1941, after the Japanese attack on the US naval base at Pearl Harbor, Hawaii. Germany declared war on the United States shortly thereafter on December 11, 1941.

As a member of the regular army, Charles Jr. was assigned to the infantry but mobilized and sent to Fort Crockett, Texas, for training as a combat aircraft crew member. Fort Crockett is on the beautiful Texas Gulf Coast near Galveston and was home of the Third Attack Group of the Army Air Corps. Charles was destined to be an aircrewman as an aerial gunner.

Charles Jr. moved from Fort Crocket to Kelly Field, San Antonio, Texas, for further training as an air crewman. Then he was transferred with his unit to New Mexico. From New Mexico, his training unit traveled to back to Texas to Ellington Field near Houston, and then back to Kelly Field in San Antonio in 1942.

6.8. B-17 Bomber USAF photo (public domain)

The service record book indicated he was training as a remote turret gun mechanic, aerial gunner, and an armorer. To be a gunner, airmen had to completely understand how guns operate and how to repair them in an emergency.

In 1941 Charles Jr. completed the marksmanship course with the .30 caliber rifle but did not qualify.

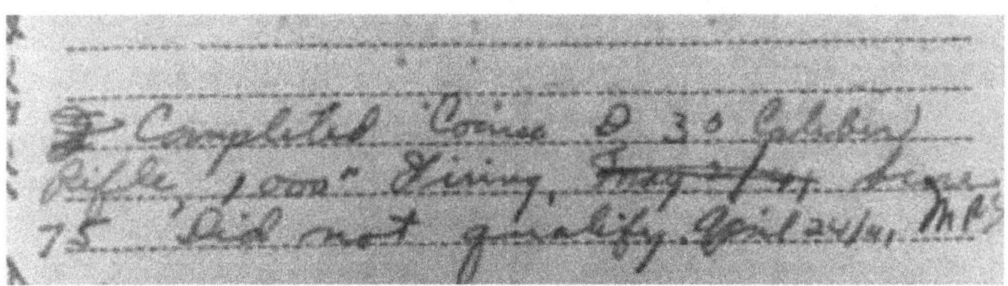

6.9. On May 24, 1941, Charles completed rifle training.

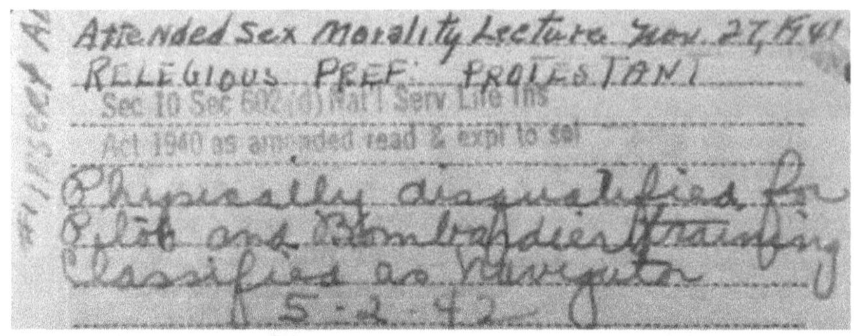

6.10. Service Record Book, disqualified for pilot and bombardier training, May 2, 1942

Charles Jr. was qualified to be a navigator but was really learning how to operate and repair the B-17's remote turret gun, the guns on top and in front of the plane. The guns in front were nicked named the "Chin" gun because of its position under the pilot's cockpit.

He also trained to be a tail gunner. A tail gunner on a B-17 rests his buttocks on a stool but is in a kneeling position facing out plexiglass viewports from the rear of the plane. The tail gunner operates twin .50 caliber machine guns that are synchronized to fire together. Enemy fighters train to approach bombers from the front above or from the rear, making the tail gunner vulnerable.

Unfortunately, during a training exercise in 1943, the plane Charles Jr. was on board crashed. He was injured and underwent treatment at three different hospitals: Denver, Colorado; Salt Lake City, Utah; and Madison, Wisconsin, all in 1943. His back was injured and he was reluctant to fly again. He made it clear, in every way possible, he was not going to be a tail gunner in a B17.

In June of 1943, Charles Jr. was enrolled in the Air Corps Technical School at Lowry Field in Denver, Colorado, with a focus on aircraft armament. His follow-on training was at Las

Vegas Army Airfield (now Nellis AFB), Nevada, to become a machine gun mechanic.

His fitness report indicated that his character was "excellent," and his efficiency rating was "satisfactory." According to his service record book (SRB), those ratings of excellent character and satisfactory in job performance followed him his entire career.

In his SRB, the Army recorded furlough November 3-12, 1943. Although he was expected to be on leave longer, he was recalled to Salt Lake on November 13, 1943. A board of officers convened, pursuant to special order 332 paragraph 29, dated November 28, 1943, Headquarters Army Air Base, Salt Lake City, Utah.

The purpose was to investigate, determine, and report on the physical condition of Pfc. Charles H. Berg Jr. and make recommendations as to whether he was physically qualified for full military duty. The board's findings were "that the subject enlisted man does not meet the minimum standards for induction under the provisions of MR19 dated October 15, 1942. Subject enlisted man was hospitalized at the Station Hospital Army Base, Salt Lake City Utah."

The board recommendations were that "the subject enlisted man be disqualified for foreign duty under the provisions of paragraph 4D circular 293 dated 11 November 1943. The subject enlisted man has been examined by the base clarification officer for reassignment to duty capable compatible with his physical disability i.e. non-skilled manual labor duty."

After the determination, the fate of his military career was doubtful. The conclusion read "duty pending."

Charles Jr. was eliminated from the Army Air Force flexible gunnery school in Las Vegas. His next physical examination in Clovis New Mexico, confirmed the findings of the previous Utah determination, that he was disqualified from flying and overseas duty on September 9, 1944.

The training mishap and his resulting conditions may have been a blessing. The life expectancy for a B-17 tail gunner in WWII was extremely low. Specific figures vary by source and period, but in late 1943, some suggest a life expectancy of around eleven missions.

B-17 Bomber in a German anti-aircraft flax field (USAF photo public domain)

Charles Jr. was again stationed at Clovis Army Airfield, New Mexico, a site for air combat training. At Clovis, the Army trained bomber and aircrews for B-17s and B-24 bombers and later the B-29s.

Charles Jr. was assigned to the 16th Bombardment Wing, who mission was to train heavy bomber crews for primarily the B-24 Liberator. Training included pilots, navigators, and gunners.

He might have been assigned to work in the armory or in the personnel office. I believe Charles spent the rest of his early duty in New Mexico in administration.

Chapter 7

Caroline Parker

HERBERT PARKER AND JOY Stitzel had one daughter: Caroline.

Caroline attended grade school in Lee Center, Illinois, and graduated from high school there in 1938. I found her grade school report cards that indicated she was an excellent student and involved in a variety of extracurricular activities including cheerleading.

Much to our chagrin, she would occasionally recite her high school cheers (circa 1938) while she was preparing dinner or sewing. Always smiling, she was keenly aware of how her leading cheers in the kitchen embarrassed us. Rummaging through old, long-forgotten, family photo albums, I found photographs of her in her ballet costume. She always enjoyed dancing.

Caroline attended the Lucille Kelly School of Dance in Dixon, Illinois. In one of the programs, she was featured in a song

7.1. *Caroline with her Morgan horse in Illinois, circa 1930s*

and dance solo and a reading of Cinderella.

Her mother, Joy, encouraged her to get involved in music, dance, sports, and riding their Morgan horses.

After high school, she was accepted at Cornell College in Mount Vernon, Iowa. She studied clothing, fabrics, and fashion design. After Cornell, she attended the Frederick Mizen Academy of Arts in Chicago.

7.2. Caroline E Parker, Cornell College 1939 yearbook

ROMANCE

Caroline was working as a clothing and fabric buyer for the prestigious Killian Company when she met Charles Jr. who was in Chicago on furlough in 1943.

Caroline was described by Charles Jr. and her brother Gordon as a "looker." She was pretty and stylish.

Charles Jr. and Caroline were immediately attracted to one another and began their lifelong romance. A love letter we found indicated she immediately discontinued her budding long-distance romance that started in 1942 with an Army first lieutenant pilot.

CHARLES BERG JR.

Charles Jr.'s training in Texas (Kelly and Ellington fields) roughly paralleled Caroline's father's (Herbert) experiences. Both were in the Army Air Service or later the Army Air Corps in bomber groups. Caroline may have believed she was getting an approximation of her father. She wasn't.

7.3. Pfc Charles H Berg Jr., 1943

Private First Class Charles Berg Jr. was a handsome man in uniform, with a ready smile and firm handshake. He had thick black hair, parted neatly on the side and plastered in place with the application of a popular cream dressing that made his hair shine.

He always dressed neatly and was proud of his appearance. He laughed and joked but was never vicious or damning with his teasing.

Not much is known about what transpired between their first meeting and their wedding. The trail went cold. I can only speculate that there were countless telephone conversations. Maybe a few clever greeting cards complete with cupid doodles and scribbled hearts and arrows. There could have been a string of love letters back and forth between the lonely months they were apart. We will never know.

Miss Parker to Be Married

Mr. and Mrs. Herbert Nichols Parker of West Brooklyn, Ill., announce the engagement and approaching marriage of their daughter, Caroline Elizabeth, to Pfc. Charles Henry Berg, jr., son of Mr. and Mrs. Charles Henry Berg of Jacksonville, Fla. The wedding will take place in Cedar Rapids sometime next month.

Miss Parker, who makes her home at 200 Thirteenth street SE, attended Cornell college in Mt. Vernon and the Fredrick Mizen Academy of Art in Chicago. She is employed as a buyer by the Killian company. Pfc. Berg is stationed at the Clovis, N. M., army air base.

7.4. Dixon Evening Telegraph, 1943

When her father suffered a serious farm accident, she returned to Lee Center to help with his recovery.

Caroline and Charles Jr. were soon engaged and scheduled a marriage ceremony in Cedar Rapids, Iowa.

The wedding was postponed because Charles Jr.'s furlough was cancelled. Still engaged to Caroline, Charles Jr. had to return to Utah. From there he was transferred back to New Mexico.

Six months later, Caroline and her mother traveled to New Mexico to solemnize the wedding.

Charles and Caroline were married in Curry County, New Mexico, in the town of Clovis on May 9, 1944.

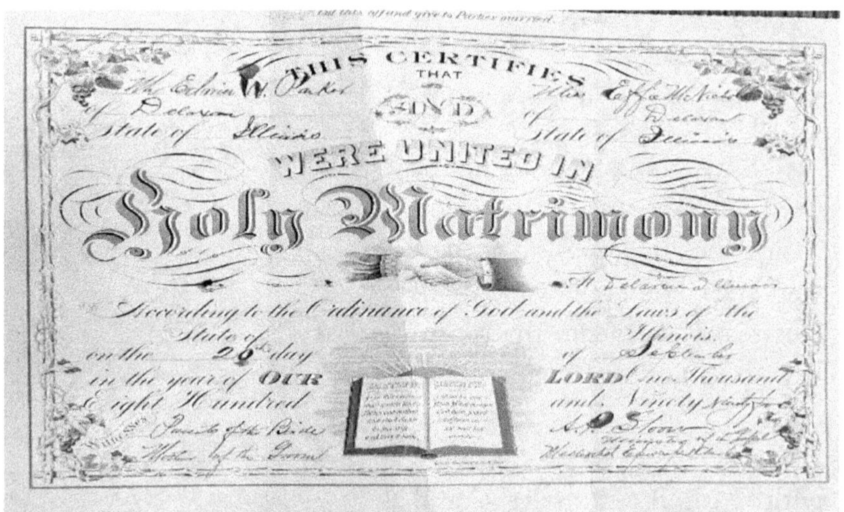

7.5. Charles H. Berg Jr. and Caroline E. Parker, married May 9, 1944

The modest ceremony was performed in the small pueblo-style St. James Episcopal church and was only attended by her mother and two other witnesses. A confirmation certificate indicates Caroline converted to Episcopalian Protestant.

Caroline returned to Illinois while Charles Jr. finished out his assignment at Clovis Airfield in New Mexico.

His next furlough was logged as August 8–29, 1944. We think that's when he returned to Illinois to move Caroline to

Florida for their next assignment.

They purchased our first house in Jacksonville, Florida.

The romance and marriage were not without issues. Charles Jr. was a son of the south and delighted in shocking his new northern relatives and later his children by preparing and eating grits, black-eyed peas, cornbread, and okra. In some ways he was a contradiction, confounding members of the northern family.

7.6. Charles, Caroline and Steve Jacksonville, Florida, first house, 1946

He enjoyed listening to classical music and blue grass banjo picking. He loved to sketch buildings and landscapes, but he also created a cartoon character that was regularly published in various Air Corps and later Air Force newspapers.

Their marriage lasted their lifetimes, but there was simmering family friction because of the geographic and cultural differences, a vestigial animosity dating back to the American Civil War.

NORTH VS. SOUTH

Charles Jr. was the only son of a fiercely loyal confederate mother, Georgia Virginia Tyler. Her first and middle names are a giveaway to her southern sympathies.

Georgia was loving, modest, and polite about her views but was deeply dedicated to the South. As children we were reminded of an often-referenced great grandfather who fought with the Florida Infantry in the Confederate Army. As young boys at a military function, when the band played a spirited rendition of the song Dixie, we were required to stand up. We never knew how serious Charles was when he proclaimed, "Save your Confederate money boys. The South will rise again."

Charles Jr. was loyal to the South and his family's military heritage. Our great-grandfather (Charles Jr.'s grandfather) William Leigh Richmond Tyler may have enlisted in Company A of the 10th Florida Infantry Regiment. He was captured by Union forces and became a prisoner of war in the battle for Petersburg, Virginia.

However, there are conflicting records regarding William Tyler. There was a militia unit organized soon after Florida's succession from the Union in Jacksonville. The Jacksonville Light Infantry was the first company to be accepted into service by the state of Florida on April 30, 1859.

That unit served as a garrison force at a battery at the mouth of the Saint Johns River where Charles Jr. had played as a young boy. Once the third Florida infantry regiment was formed, the Jacksonville Light Infantry was mustered in as Company A of the regiment on August 10th, 1861. The muster of Company A of the 10th Florida Infantry does not list William L. R. Tyler.

By 1863 Union forces were occupying positions along the St. Johns River. In fact, the records show a regiment of the 144th New York Volunteers boarded a transport, the *Harriet A. Weed*, and relocated several miles down the St. Johns River.

The complete story of William Tyler remains a mystery, but we know our great-grandfather fought for the Confederacy.

Dr. Silas Parker for the North

Let's backtrack for a moment in order to put things in perspective. Caroline's father Herbert Parker was the son of Edwin Parker (discussed in Chapter 2). Silas was Edwin's father.

Silas was a northern Civil War doctor who tended to the needs of his fellow soldiers during the bloody Civil War. This is his obituary.

Doctor Silas Parker was born in Meigs County, Ohio and died in Delavan on April 9, 1879, at the age of 59 years and 11 months. He was a practicing physician in Delavan for 24 years. During his life here he enjoyed the implicit confidence of the people both as an upright citizen and eminent physician. He was a man of simple ways, and his patience always found him as kind and sympathetic a friend as he was a skilled physician. His funeral was held at Presbyterian Church.

7.7. Dr Silas Parker, Civil War Surgeon, circa 1865

Silas Parker served as First Lieutenant Company H 115th Regiment of Illinois volunteer infantry. Lieutenant Parker was so overcome by the sorrow because of the death of an only son he felt just to the government required his resignation which he tendered March 12, 1868. He then returned to Delavan and resumed the practice of medicine but lived only a few years.

Caroline was subtly labeled by her southern in-laws as the Yankee daughter of loyal northerners.

Chapter 8

A Military Family

Charles Jr. enjoyed talking about his youth in Florida and serving out his enlistment as an information specialist, his new military occupational specialty while stationed in Florida.

Florida

WWII ended in August of 1945 with Charles Jr. remaining in continental US. He wasn't forward deployed to the theater in Europe or in the Pacific. In 1949 he underwent a physical examination at Fort McPheron, Georgia, for the purpose of "Disch." (discharge) from the Army Air Corps.

The military experienced a reduction in force. Staff Sargent Berg was discharged from the active-duty service "at convenience of the government" in November of 1950.

The US became involved in the Korean war on June 27, 1950. He was reactivated in 1951, and in 1952, he was transferred to England without his family.

8.1. Charles to England on board the USNA Stewart, 1952

8.2. Charles Jr. before the family arrived in England, 1952

Our family lived in Jacksonville near his parents until we could be reunited.

While Charles Jr. primarily played with bows and arrows when he was young, I was given my first gun at an early age. Of course, we also had our bows and arrows.

8.3. George Jacksonville, Florida, 1950

8.4. Charles Jr. bought us guns, bows and arrows. Jacksonville, Florida, 1951

Caroline, my brother Steve, and I joined Charles Jr. in late 1952 in England. We sailed across the Atlantic Ocean on the USS *Washington*.

8.5. Transatlantic crossing, USS Washington, 1952

8.6. George and Steve, crossing the Atlantic, February, 1952

In 1953, after multiple background checks, Charles received a top secret national security clearance.

ENGLAND

When we arrived in England there was no military housing for American service member's families. We lived on the local economy, first in an apartment in London, then we moved into a beautiful cottage in Gerrards Cross.

8.7. The village of Gerrards Cross, England, 1953

8.8. Charles Jr. and Steve in Gerrards Cross Cottage next to 1953 Volkswagen

Our final move was to a twenty-three-room estate in Chalfont St. Peter, which was in a ritzy neighborhood outside London.

8.9. The house in Chalfont St Peter, London England, 1953

England and most of Europe had been destroyed for the most part. American GIs and Airmen brought welcome dollars that stimulated the British economies. My parents could afford an Italian nanny and an English housekeeper; it was luxurious.

8.10. Caroline, nanny, George, and Steve; London, 1952-53

As small boys at the house in Chalfont St Peter, we would eagerly wait for the milkman by gate of our long driveway leading to the main road. The milkman had a wagon pulled by a monstrous draft horse. The cart had large, steel-rimmed, wooden wheels that made a grinding sound with each turn. The friendly clip-clop of the horseshoes on the cobblestone road was unmistakable. We ran as fast as we could when we heard it.

The platform of the cart was lined with milk bottles that clacked when it moved. Low to the ground, the cart was easy for the driver (and my older brother and I) to get on and off. Smiling, we hitched rides with him that summer. He would tell either one of us to go to the next house, take the fresh bottles of whole milk, and pick up the empty bottles.

Fresh whole milk, cream rising to the top, was delivered to insulated coolers by the back doors of each of the houses. I thought it was fantastic, so did the stocky milkman. He got to rest with the horse as his miniature American blokes performed his morning chores. A tap on the head and a "That's a good lad," and we were off the next house.

London was exciting for my older brother and me. We were oblivious to the changes in the culture or the pace of the recovery after WWII.

In 1953, Queen Elizabeth II was crowned in Westminster Abbey and Edmund Hillary and Sherpa Tensing became the first people to scale the summit of Mount Everest.

But everyday life for the ordinary citizen in Britain was, by the standards of today, quite simple. It was all about change. For the first time since the war, petrol was unrationed and a huge influx of cars took to the roads. The new cars were very state-of-the-art, but they still didn't come fitted with seat belts.

The relatively quiet country lanes became more congested, so major new roads were being planned to stretch to all parts of the country. By the end of the decade, a new word was entered into the English Dictionary: motorways. By 1953, rationing had ceased, and the clothes that the average person wore were very different to those worn before the war.

Everybody smoked and there was historically bad, even lethal, coal smog. Young boys at school wore short trousers and knee-length socks and peaked school caps were obligatory. Television sets started to appear, taking up their now-familiar place as the focal point of the living room, and outside, strange-looking aerials were clamped firmly to chimney stacks.

Some things hadn't changed at all though; murderers were still hanged for their crimes, and pubs closed at ten p.m. as usual. Looking back to 1953, life perhaps appeared hard, but it did have several good points. There was virtually no vandalism, swearing in public places was an offense, and gentlemen still gave up their seats to ladies on buses and trams.

In 1953, London was a city in a complex period of recovery and transition following World War II, simultaneously defined by lingering austerity and burgeoning optimism. London was exciting and recovering from WWII.

8.11. George, Tower of London guard, Steve; London, 1952

My dad's ability to find unique living circumstances went under appreciated until we realized the effort it took to find housing in neighborhoods that would enrich our lives. We thought it was normal and that everybody had the same fantastic experiences. We walked to Regents and Hyde Parks, rode the red double-decker buses, and toured the Tower of London.

Steve attended an exclusive private Episcopal school (Hampton Gurney) while I went to school on base for military dependents.

Charles Jr. and Caroline's third son Malcolm Ross, a future airman, was born while we were in England.

Dad was an information tech, dealing with public relations and writing newspaper and magazine articles for the Air Force. His byline was often "an Air Force spokesman says."

8.12. Steve in his Hampton Gurney School uniform (and an orange popsicle), 1953

8.13. A family portrait posed for a magazine article about life in the US Air Force in England, 1953

I found an article in a British newspaper describing life for American families.

Take S. Ruislip for example, where the Third Air Force has its headquarters. Four years ago, it was a quiet, little, middle-class suburb near London. Today it's Little America in the midst of England. A typical South Ruislip American family is Sergeant Charles Berg, 34, of Jacksonville, Florida, his wife Connie, 31, and their two husky boys, Steve six and George four.

Berg is a soft-spoken southerner with 12 years in the Air Force who finds life almost like stateside. During the weather though he says with a grin, "We use kerosene, electric, and coal heaters—even the kitchen gas stove—to try to keep warm, but we had to give that up now. We'll just keep one room warm and use the rest of the house as an ice box."

Like most middle-class suburban homes in England, the Bergs seven room, $100 a month, furnished residence has no central heating.

Caroline misses the shopping back home but is getting used to making changes in English money and standing in line at a half-dozen different stores to buy what she needs. Like other Air Force families in England, sparse food rationing, which often limits each person to one egg a week, doesn't affect the Bergs very much. They draw most of their food from the base commissary and post exchange.

Little Stephen at first went to the local Church of England parochial school but had to knuckle under to some pretty strict discipline. Now Steve, like most other airmen's children, attends an American school run by the Air Force. Like any school back home, little Stephen and his brother George fit easily into the neighborhood life. They show their English playmates some of the finer points of Cowboys and Indians. In return the English boys show the Berg boys how to play conkers in which horse chestnuts are tied on the end of strings and knock together.

Charles drops in about two nights a week at the local pub, the Jolly Farmer, for a pint or two of ale (before the family arrived). "After they had seen me coming in for about a month, I earned my first 'Good evening,'" said Charles. "Now I'm one of the regulars. I even played darts once in a while."

The English neighbors are friendly. When the Bergs moved in, local housewives paid a formal call. The Bergs were invited out for tea and crumpets. They returned the invitation with coffee and sandwiches. Now they get together quite often. Both Caroline and Charles agree the biggest Anglo-American problem is the lonely American airman with no family and nowhere to go when he's off duty.

8.14. Steve, George, and Big Ben Clock; London, England, 1953

The entire family enjoyed England; we became Anglophiles, enjoying tea and crumpets with marmalade or chutney.

The sound of Bagpipes still stirs our souls. The deep chime of the clock Big Ben is unforgettable.

We witnessed Queen Elizabeth II's coronation (1953) and visited many classic landmarks all over England, e.g. Westminster Abbey, Stonehenge, Tower of London, the changing of the guard at Windsor Castle, and others.

When our tour of duty was up, we sailed from England on the American ship the USS *Rose* for our next US Air Force family adventure.

8.15. Caroline and Malcolm on board the USS Rose returning from England, 1954

8.16. Steve and George playing shuffleboard aboard the USS Rose leaving England, 1954

PENNSYLVANIA

Our next duty station was Olmsted Air Force Base, near Harrisburg and Middletown Pennsylvania in 1954.

The 147th Flight Service Squadron at Military Air Transport Service (MATS) supported operations of flights during the 1948-1949 Berlin airlift. The US supply depot at Olmsted AFB provided emergency support supplies for the airlift operations.

Charles Jr. was in information technology (public relations) and worked as an Air Force recruiter. As always, he managed to find great places for us to live. For this assignment, the family leased a house on a rural dairy farm.

8.17. Dairy farm in rural Pennsylvania, running the farmer's Irish Setter for exercise, 1954

We explored the nearby stream for miles. The stream that lazily flowed through the farm and nearby woods was where we learned to swim. We helped raise the Irish Setter puppies the farmer bred. The farmer welcomed us shooting pigeons with our BB guns in the hay barn and milking parlor.

When that tour of duty was concluded, we moved south to Virgina and Maryland. But it was the farm in Pennsylvania that reminded us of our agrarian roots.

MARYLAND

In 1955 Charles Jr. was working as an information technician at Andrews Air Force Base in Washington, DC, for the 85th Air Division Headquarters and lived in Maryland. In 1958, he transferred to the Washington Air Defense Sector (WaADS) at Fort Lee, Virginia, to be the noncommissioned-officer-in-charge of information services. The WaADS was established in December 1956 as the 4625th Air Defense Wing, providing command and control over several aircraft, missile, and radar squadrons along the eastern seaboard.

That summer, Steve and I spent time on the farm in Illinois with our mother's family, ostensibly learning how to work. Our grandparents took us on a road trip to Michigan to a fish camp where we met Uncle George. He was quiet, introspective, and interested in hearing about our travels. Most of all, he wanted to know about his sister Caroline.

I sensed the respect and affection between the brother and sister. George enlisted in the Army Air Corps during WWII, but I could not determine what his job was or where he served. Apparently, there was animosity with some of the bigoted relatives because George married a Catholic girl and moved to Michigan after the war.

We first lived in College Park, Maryland, and went to local grade schools there. On January 29, 1956, our sister Elizabeth Ann Berg was born

8.18. Uncle George Parker, 1955

at Walter Reed Army Hospital, Maryland (basically Washington, DC).

Charles Jr. said with pride that he finally got a daughter and was glad that she was born south of the Mason-Dixon line, the historic symbolic boundary between the northern and southern states.

Charles Jr. was transferred to a new assignment at Andrews Air Force Base that required us to relocate to Virgina.

8.19. Elizabeth home from the Walter Reed Hospital, Maryland, 1956

VIRGINIA

Our first house was in the country near Hopewell, Virginia. It was an old plantation estate that was registered in Richmond, Virginia, in 1729. The ancient, colonial-style, red brick house with gabled dormers witnessed the birth of the nation.

8.20. The Plantation near Hopewell, Virginia, 1959

It experienced the bloody battles of the Civil War. A giant magnolia tree graced the circular driveway that was overgrown years ago with weeds and vines.

Charles Jr. was a student of the Civil War. On weekends we traveled to different battlefield monuments. Dad could recite from memory the details of the fight, usually emphasizing the Confederate soldiers. The siege of Petersburg had a special significance for him. His grandfather fought there and was captured by the Union forces.

By now in his Air Force career, Charles Jr. was confident presenting talks in public to various audiences, a consummate professional.

But not at the Civil War Memorial at Petersburg. He would pause and choke up describing the slaughter, then fold his arms across his chest and stare out beyond the reconstructed grass covered revetments. He knew the end of the Civil War and victory for the North was all but confirmed at the Battle of Petersburg. As children, we didn't understand any of it. We ran and jumped around as if it was a regular playground.

At our plantation home after a hard rain, we would rush to the fields to find Indian arrowheads and recently exposed shell fragments and lead bullets from both sides of the Civil War. We had cigar boxes full of Civil War relics.

There were no streetlights, television, or road noise. On clear, cloudless nights, we lay in the cool grass and counted shooting stars.

The absentee owners raised peanuts, corn, and watermelon in the exhausted sandy fields. The crops were tended to and harvested by Black workers we hardly ever saw. We gleaned peanuts from the fields for Caroline to roast. The earthy fragrance of the roasted peanuts filled the lofty ceilings throughout the entire house.

At Christmas time, we cut down a handsome pine tree from the thick forest in the back of the plantation and pulled it home on a sled. The entire house had a clean, fresh, pine scent. We never wanted to take the tall tree down, and we didn't until long passed New Year's Eve.

We adopted a few stray dogs. Our favorite was a mangy three-legged one we named Long John Silver after the peg-legged pirate in the novel *Treasure Island* by Robert Louis Stephenson.

The historic farm had a resident horse and a pony (Trixie and Dixie) that we were invited by the landlord to care for. We did and rode them mostly bareback. They were agreeable but herd-bound and barn-sour. They didn't like being separated or our taking long trail rides in the Virginia summer heat.

My older brother and I decided to harness Trixie to an old, dusty, black buggy we found in a rundown shed. It probably hadn't been moved in decades. We were going to tour the farm in style, driving the once beautiful buggy. The old bay horse deeply resented being trussed in the worn leather collar and dried out carriage tack. She pinned her ears straight back as we carefully arranged the brittle leather equipment.

When we got all the rigging attached, we slowly mounted the wooden bench seat and gathered the reins. One giddy up and Trixie kicked and bucked the ancient carriage into small pieces. Traumatically and forcefully dismounted, we carefully unharnessed her, gathering the fragments of the buggy into a pile. Dad apologized to the landlord and offered restitution, but he settled for, "I'm very sorry about the buggy."

The gravel driveway to the old mansion house ran about a half mile to the rural paved road. There was no noise at night except for the owls and the barking of a few stray dogs. Steve and I loved to explore the outbuildings that were dilapidated, including the antebellum slave quarters. We fantasized about what life was like in the 1860s.

Creeping through the outbuildings, we listened as the gray, weathered, wooden siding on the old structures creaked and cracked when the wind blew through boards. They were neglected and in disrepair.

We played in the ancient smokehouse that was filled with bones and skulls of cattle and hogs, our imaginations created satanic voodoo spirits. Our water was pumped from a deep well to a wood-staved tower that provided water pressure for the entire house. The water line to the house froze on extremely frigid days. Mom melted snow to cook with. We took sponge baths from a warm bucket of water.

Fort Lee

In 1958, we moved to the nearby Army post and lived in government housing (building 440 G) on Fort Lee in Virgina. Now more civilized, we explored the training venues used by the US Army. My brothers and I collected spent shell casing and links after maneuvers and constructed our own machine gun ammunition belts. The final length of one of our machine gun belts was nine feet long.

We shadowed training mission, crawled on the ground with the young soldiers, and annoyed the sergeants and corporals by sneaking into various educational venues, including parachute training towers, the outdoor classroom bleachers, and training bunkers. Most of the private trainees just smiled and shooed us away.

We loved living in Virginia surrounded by the history, civility, and classy dogwood ambiance of that part of the South.

8.21. Steve and George waiting on baggage claim with Grandma Joy Parker. Probably leaving Virginia, circa 1960s

GERMANY

Our next duty station was Germany. On this transatlantic journey, we flew from Virginia to New Jersey to Ireland then to Frankfurt Main, Germany. Frankfurt is the primary terminal for arriving dependents. We were to be stationed on the largest North Atlantic Treaty Organization (NATO) base in Europe—Ramstein Air Base.

Ramstein Air Base is in the southwestern German state of Rhineland-Pfalz. It's part of the Kaiserslautern military community—the largest military community outside the US. The community includes Landstuhl, Kaiserslautern, and smaller towns and villages surrounding the base. Ramstein Air base was originally built by the French in 1950 but subsequently became an American base by 1952. The area is the main wine grape-growing region of Germany. It is also known for being the largest connected forest, which as young boys, we explored almost daily.

In Charles Jr.'s annual medical exam at the 86th Tactical Hospital on Ramstein Air Base, Germany, he listed his local home address as Waldstrasse, Weltersbach. Translated from German, *Waldstrasse* is wooded or forest street and in the village of mill stream, Weltersbach.

We enjoyed living off base with the German families. Our small village was close to the town of Steinwenden (stone pasture in English), where there were larger shops. We could walk over an ancient stone bridge that crossed a fast-moving stream to visit. A timeless sense of permanence was set with the ever-present ancient stone buildings.

Our house was the newest one in the small village.

8.22. Sitting on the highest point in the area, the house overlooked the valley below.

8.23. Hilltop view from our house in Weltersbach, 1963

In the mornings, we walked down to the school bus station on a narrow cobblestone road, past the tiny gray brick and cut stone houses of the villagers. We often waved to the farmers harnessing their horses as they began their day's chores. They grew potatoes and wheat, fertilizing the row crops with "honey wagons" pulled by a team of horses or small tractors that sprayed fermented raw human sewage. It only smelled disgusting for a few days until the sunlight killed the bacteria, but we never walked or played in those fields.

In the winter an old German lady befriended us. She was bent over with age with a shawl draped over shoulders and her gray hair covered with a scarf tied under her chin. She invited us into her small stone house by the school bus stop to get warm. On her small wood and coal burning stove, she invariably had potatoes (*Kartoffels*) boiling. We loved the smell of her tiny kitchen.

On rare occasions, she could afford to make apple strudel (*Apfelstrudel*). She joyfully shared whatever she baked with "her" three American boys, especially if we brought apples picked from the orchard behind our house.

She was always smiling and accommodating. I noticed a crumpled yellowing certificate hanging by a nail on her plastered wall. It had an image of an iron cross and at the bottom a small swastika—the symbol of the Nazi Germany. She noticed my interest and she cautiously pulled open the drawer of her wooden hutch (*Kuchenregal*). In the drawer were WWII German army medals, lapel pins, old Third Reich German coins and ribbons. With a trusting smile she let me pick out a few now useless Nazi Deutsche *Marks* and *Pfennige* for my coin collection.

A one-room shop across from her house sold multicolored gummi bears (*Gummbarchen or Gummibar*) that we bought with spare change in German money we found on our dad's dresser.

In the evenings, some of the villagers walked up the hill to the national forest to socialize and exercise (*spaziergang* or *abendgang*). A few looked our way and smiled; most minded their own business. They strolled along the path that bordered the field near our house and the state-owned forest. The group was usually led by a well-dressed man with a long staff, who would wave and smile. He was the village mayor (*Burgermeister*) and owned our house.

8.24. The entrance to the state owned forest next to our house, Germany, 1963

On a chilly fall evening, someone from the village placed a shivering, tiny, German Shepherd puppy on our doorstep. She could fit in a shoebox and was cold and hungry. So, now we had a dog; we named her Nora.

She followed us everywhere and blended into the family, developing an intense bond particularly with my older brother and me. She enjoyed not being collared and was seldom leashed. When we moved on to the Air Force base, she came with us.

Fireworks were cheap, and we spent time detonating them wherever and whenever we could. We explored the

8.25. Nora, our gift from the villagers in Weltersbach, Germany, 1963

countryside and were never scolded when we crossed a fence or ventured onto private farms. We were those *Amerikanisch* or *Amerikaner kinder.* I'm not sure if they minded or not. After all, they may have thought we were harmless, or they feared the conquering warriors' sons.

8.26. One of the many cathedrals we visited in Germany, 1963

On weekends we always visited a new place in our family's two-tone blue, 1956 Chevrolet, four-door Belaire. Very often the attraction was an enormous castle or cathedral ironically spared during the carpet bombing by the Army Air Corps.

Christmas in Germany for a child is mesmerizing. Every small town and city had colorful Christmas decorations. Festive music was broadcast from cozy stores. Eating handfuls of hot roasted chestnuts or a warm salted pretzel wrapped in brown paper was a treat. The details designed into hand crafted German toys created lifelong memories, all courtesy of the USAF.

We eventually moved onto Ramstein Air Base, into a second-story, three-bedroom apartment. We walked to school and had more American friends. Playing marbles was the primary sport. Everyone had a bag of cat eye glass or German agate stone marbles. A small circle was scratched into the dirt with a stick. The players put a few of their marbles into the ring, and we took turns trying to knock them out of the dirt circle. Having a particular shooter was important. It was usually slightly larger than the rest of the marbles and had hundreds of tiny chips taken out of it from constant use that made it easier to flick from your thumb. With practice, the velocity of the shooter was enough to knock several marbles out of the ring, which you got to keep.

The American Youth Activities (AYA) center had a jukebox, pool tables, and ping pong tables. But it was supervised and too tame. Going to the base gym and harassing the airmen playing basketball or watching judo and boxing matches was a great pastime. As spectators, we learned just by watching and imitating them.

There were ample opportunities to get into trouble on and off base if you had adventurous friends. I think members of my gang (the "hard guys") either ended up in prison, as USAF fighter pilots, or CEO of large corporations.

Our oldest brother was studious and did well in his classes. I did not. I was a committed delinquent and ran with the "wrong" crowd. The mischief was seriously criminal in some cases, but I was never caught—only accused. Running to escape from the young airmen police (APs or "Apes") was a sport. The real danger was, if you were caught, your father would be the one who could feel the repercussions through reduction in rank or even sent back to the States.

Our family dog Nora enjoyed her walks on base (now collared and leashed) but still retained her snarling and growling defense of the family. She was a German Sheppard and that is their nature. We lived near the boundary of the base and occasionally we walked in the forest to find old German ammunition dumps filled with unexploded bullets, artillery shells, and other war relics. We emptied the corroded cartridges, poured out the purple potassium permanganate, and lit it on fire. (Toward the end of the war, the Germans didn't have the ingredients to be able to make high quality gunpowder).

Also in the forest were German kids and their dogs. Once, a German gang member released the leash on his large, solid, black male dog. It attacked Nora and got the best of her. Infuriated, I picked up a big stick and beat the German kid until he called off his dog. Satisfied, I took pleasure in defending our beautiful small brown and black Nora.

Tragically, she nipped our father's commanding officer's daughter when their family visited our apartment. Two days later, a white, enclosed van pulled up. Two very polite and respectful air policemen led Nora on a leash to the truck. She calmly and without hesitation jumped in the back of the police van, and she was gone.

Sometimes we went with Dad to his office on Saturdays and reviewed newsreels he was going to be introducing. My favorite was his introduction of the F-104 fighter jet with his opening line, "The new sound of freedom—the Lockheed F-104 Starfighter."

8.27. F-104s (US Air Force photo, National Museum of the U.S. Air Force, public domain)

Then he would start the flickering reel-to-reel film projector. The stuttering sound of his Bell & Howell "movie machine" and the drawn office curtains were our cues to be quiet and listen. As the NCOIC with access to the office, he showed us military films and occasionally narrated and explained the newsreels.

My favorites reels were propaganda films about Navy ships and the Marine Corps. The series was called "Victory at Sea." Watching those Navy newsreels, I imagined what it would be like to be on a ship in rough seas or storming a beach as a Marine.

Dad had a shiny scale model of the F-104 on his desk. The exact replica of the real plane was most likely a promotional gift from Lockheed who designed and built the actual plane. We were not supposed to play with it, but it was tempting to young boys. A few days after delivering a blistering correction for touching the desk ornament, Dad came home with the Revell Company plastic model kit. We assembled and painted it together. After that, I built almost every model, plastic airplane in the Air Force's arsenal.

We loved going to work with him and meeting the international military folks at the NATO base in Ramstein in 1963.

8.28. Charles Jr. (third from the left) and the International NATO Team , Ramstein, Germany, 1963

Few young boys got to have dinner in the upscale French officers' club in Baden-Baden with a wing commander's family or eat a hot dog in the bleachers at a baseball game with Leopold III, the king of Belgium.

Germany was a wonderful, exciting experience, and we were reluctant to rotate out of the assignment. From Germany, we moved to Georgia in 1964. Sadly, our time as US Air Force dependents would soon to be over.

GEORGIA

In 1964, Charles Jr. was stationed on Dobbins Air Force Base, located in Cobb County, outside Atlanta, near the city of Marietta, Georgia. Marietta is a suburb twenty miles northwest of Atlanta. The reserve base hosted the 94th Airlift Wing of the Air Force Reserve Command and its fleet of C-130 Hercules aircraft. The base was shared off and on with elements of the Army, Navy and Marine Corps. As a reserve base, the operational tempo seemed less hectic than other duty stations we were assigned to.

Our first quarters were a two-bedroom motel that was cramped and uncomfortable. It was miserable. We stayed there about two weeks until Dad found a house for the family.

Finally, we moved into a comfortable, brick house in a quiet neighbor in nearby Smyrna, Georgia. Steve was about to graduate from high school early. He was seventeen. I was in junior high. Malcolm and Elizabeth were in grade school.

Military families experience a variety of world cultures and learn to be tolerant and open minded. It's a requirement for family life in the US Air Force. However, we landed in the segregated South. It was unusual for us to be enrolled in White-only schools. I was shocked when a classmate whispered that she secretly enjoyed, but was ashamed of, listening to "their music." She was referring to Black Americans.

While we were in Germany, we listened to Radio Luxembourg. The station was a major source of pop music and entertainment for listeners all over Europe. In 1963, Radio Luxembourg launched a program called "Music in the Night."

The American radio station stopped broadcasting and "signed off" in the evening. To listen to the latest music, we would crowd around the radio and enthusiastically listen to rock 'n roll music as if it were our only contact with the outside world (there was no television). Radio Luxembourg attracted a large audience nightly of more than a million people. The station boasted the most powerful, privately owned transmitter in Europe—200 kW on long wave.

In 1963, Radio Luxembourg was considered an underground station because it broadcasted new hits and fledgling artists like The Rolling Stones and Elvis Presley. Thanks to the station, we had already been listening to musicians like Otis Redding, The Drifters, The Ronettes, and the Chiffons when we arrived in Georgia. It was astounding to us that those Black rock 'n roll entertainers were rejected by our southern friends because of their race.

One of Dad's strict rules was absolutely no bigotry, racial slurs, or any form of intolerance. The other rule was that no bullying was allowed. Any hint of a breach from one of us and the rule was instantaneously enforced. In Georgia, we routinely heard the forbidden derogatory word for African Americans.

As Air Force children, we were adaptable and adjusted to the all-White world in Georgia. Over time however, our mother was deeply offended by the overt racist culture. I was in the high school auditorium at an assembly when the principal announced tearfully that President John F. Kennedy had been assassinated. JFK was the first Catholic President and a Yankee from Boston. While the principal was describing the tragedy and dismissing classes for the rest of the day, he was drowned out by the loud celebratory cheers of the students and some of the gleeful faculty. However, many of the teachers, unashamed, openly sobbed.

The high school rednecks harassed our older brother Steve. He was a national merit scholar and prodigiously read about philosophy, history, and art. He spoke fluent German and got As in Latin. He talked *funny* as a Yankee and was not athletic; he didn't fit in. But one of his history teachers (Mrs. Ross) understood his character and took a liking to him. She often invited him to her house to learn about southern history and manners, teaching him in her dignified magnolia drawl.

Steve graduated early from high school and escaped to Atlanta to study at the Art Institute there. He stayed a student his entire life.

One of the pivotal incidences of our time in Georgia was a twilight march by the Ku Klux Klan. As children, we wanted to see the silent parade, so on our knees, we peered through the blades of the venetian blinds. With flaming torches, they slowly paraded down the darkening road in front of our house on their way to a nearby rally. It was frightening as the torches created eerie shadows on their sharply pointed hoods and white robes. Charles angerly told us—in no uncertain terms—to get away from the windows. We had to hide. It was searing, sinister, and unforgettable.

Illinois

Caroline asked Charles Jr. to request a transfer out of Georgia, and he agreed. Billets were limited. He was offered a reenlistment and a four-year contract for a tour of duty to England. When he announced the new assignment, Caroline protested. She was tired of the incessant movement and relocation. She was not going to England again. In 1965, she decided to take the family to Dixon, Illinois, where we would be comfortable near her extended family, but our nuclear family was separated. For the next three years, there was not a father in our home. He was a ghost.

After his time in England, Dad returned to the States from his last duty station and retired from the Air Force. He rejoined the family. Now home, he relished time with his daughter Elizabeth and especially enjoyed being a vocal fan at soon-to-be Airman Malcolm's athletic and sporting events. Charles Jr. ended his career in the US Air Force in 1966.

He accomplished a great deal in his twenty-six-year career. He had joined the Army Air Service, which became the Army Air Corps, and finally evolved into the United States Air Force.

He trained as a clerk, briefly as an infantry soldier, machine gun mechanic, as a gunner, and as an aircrew member. He worked as an information specialist in public relations and as a recruiter. He even spent a brief time as a chaplain assistant.

Charles Jr. loved his family and his service in the Air Force. He and the US Air Force provided exciting and enriching experiences for all of us. He especially loved his wife, Caroline. Throughout their entire US Air Force adventure and for the rest of their lives, they stayed dedicated to one another.

Their third son Malcolm was the one to carry on the US Air Force tradition.

SECTION 3

Chapter 9

Malcolm R. Berg

MY BROTHER MALCOLM BERG was born on March 23, 1953, at the US Naval Hospital, Middlesex, England. He was baptized as an Episcopalian in the same heirloom christening gown all of us wore. As older brothers, Steve and I watched the ceremony in the magnificent St. Paul's Cathedral in London. As a toddler in England, Malcolm was looked after by our Italian nanny and an English lady who took care of the house.

Malcolm was precocious and naturally curious. He was interested in toy lead soldiers made by British craftsmen. As an adult, he collected them along with stamps from all over the world. He had a penchant for detail and precision.

I joined the Boy Scouts of America, but Steve did not. Malcolm followed suit by joining the Cub Scouts while we were in Germany. Mom was the assistant den mother and made sure he was dressed appropriately for meetings and volunteered to supervise activities.

As older brothers, Steve and I were to ensure he met his potential. We drilled into him the subject matter associated with obtaining arrowheads, i.e. merit badges. With no television and while living among the Germans, teaching Malcolm was rewarding for him and entertaining for us. He was awarded so many arrowheads; he was investigated by the Boy Scouts of America organization.

9.1. Malcolm Berg Germany, 1959

Two representatives visited our house to verify he was doing the required work. He was legit—we made certain, as we acted as teachers and disciplinarians. The investigators left the house muttering to themselves.

In Virginia, we regularly hiked to the back of the property and beyond; Malcolm kept up. He became resilient and tougher, having the pace set by his brothers.

Because Malcolm was six and eight years younger than we were, he developed his own interests and friends. He loved baseball, but Steve and I didn't. He was a very fast runner. He excelled and set a local Little League record for stolen bases. "But I'm sure it's been broken," Malcolm says.

Once retired, Charles often watched Malcolm's baseball games from a folding aluminum chair in front of the family car near center field.

9.2. Malcolm Little League, 1960

Malcolm loved all things baseball and was enamored with science, military toys, and games. He went to Lincoln and

Madison grade school in Dixon, Illinois, and made lifelong friends there.

Malcolm attended the architecturally beautiful Dixon High School nestled on the banks of the relentlessly slow Rock River. A good athlete, he played football for three years, skipping his junior year to play music.

He got mostly As and Bs in college-prep classes and had an independent, rebellious nature, running with a crowd he called the "Razzers." Holding down different jobs

9.3. Malcolm as defensive end Dixon High School, 1970

throughout high school, he was frugal spending his money, a characteristic that lasted a lifetime. Popular and well-liked, he was voted president of his senior class and played on the winning 1970 football team.

Malcolm was industrious; when not playing music or sports, he was working for spending money. Our parents consistently praised him for mowing the lawn or otherwise helping around the house. Malcolm enjoyed singing in the church choir at St. Lukes Episcopal Church in Dixon.

After football ended in his senior year, my brother followed the fad of the counterculture epoch and grew his hair long, wore faded jeans, and had a suede jacket with long fringe on the sleeves. If you didn't know him, one might have mistaken him for a hippie musician. He played guitar and formed various groups calling themselves by different eclectic names.

Patterning his musical style after the contemporary group Crosby, Stills, Nash, and Young, Malcolm spent hours—even days—upstairs in his room practicing his guitar.

In the fall of 1967 when Malcolm was a sophomore in high school, I joined the Marine Corps as an infantry rifleman and volunteered to go to Vietnam. I was wounded

9.4. Malcolm Berg, senior photo, 1971

and spent four months in various hospitals. I was discharged in 1969 and returned to Dixon.

During Malcolm's junior year (1970), over four hundred college campus were shut down by rioters protesting the war in Vietnam and racial inequality, led by the Black Panther group. Disruptive social justice warriors roamed college campuses. The Stonewall Gay Bar riot revealed the oppression of that divergent subculture. Radical feminism and communist-inspired revolutionaries protested the draft, the military, and the government in general. The radical anarchist group the Weatherman Underground exploded a bomb in the US capital. There was a cultural revolution underway. It may have been potentially safer to avoid college and military service.

Malcolm graduated from high school in May 1971 and spent the summer working and contemplating his future. He took music theory and introduction to chemistry at the local junior college and passed with an A in each. Although he could have, he didn't want to go to college immediately after high school.

The war in Vietnam was still lethal to American soldiers, Marines, and airmen in 1971 when Malcolm enlisted. The Air Force was actively bombing the enemy (Operation Linebacker) from bases in Vietnam and Thailand.

Following the example of his grandfather and father, Malcolm joined the United States Air Force. In August of 1971, he quietly and without fanfare said goodbye to his family and close friends. With a gym bag, twenty dollars and his dad's wristwatch, he arrived at Lackland Air Force Base, San Antonio, Texas.

9.5. Malcolm Berg, boot camp, Lackland AFB, Texas, 1971

TEXAS

Malcolm did well in basic training, having played football in high school, but he reported that south Texas was "very hot."

He had long wanted to be a military medic, so he applied to and was accepted into the initial medical training, which he completed in October 1971. Due to the drawdown in Vietnam, fewer medics were needed, so he was offered cross-training as a dental technician. Malcolm completed technical school at Sheppard Air Force Base in Wichita Falls, Texas, in February 1972. After a brief visit to Dixon, he was assigned to duty in Germany.

GERMANY

Malcolm's first duty assignment after technical school was Wiesbaden Regional Hospital, Germany. He enjoyed Germany again and served at that duty station from February 1972 until August 1975.

Malcolm made beneficial use of the opportunities offered by the Air Force. He studied the German language and traveled extensively throughout Europe. The University of Maryland had an education extension program on base, so Malcolm took a variety of undergraduate college classes at night after work. He accumulated classroom credit hours that were transferable to other universities stateside.

9.6. Airman First Class Malcolm, Wiesbaden, Germany, 1972

In 1973, Malcolm was sent to Russia for six-weeks temporary duty (TDY) in Moscow at the US embassy. He studied Russian with a former prisoner in the Soviet Gulag, a cell mate of the dissident Russian author Solzhenitsyn. Malcolm's Russian was good enough to exchange pleasant greetings and to order vodka to drink with diplomats from a variety of countries.

9.7. Staff Sargeant Berg, Moscow, Russia, 1973

Part of the dental service's TDY mission, besides treating embassy employees and diplomats, was to spirit-in sensitive, espionage listening devices cloaked as dental supplies and new equipment.

In 1974, he was selected as the youngest, outstanding staff sergeant in the US Air Force. Malcolm was on the fast track to success in the Air Force with a sharp vertical trajectory. He was confident and self-possessed; he knew where he was going. He was labeled a "fast burner," an Air Force term for exceptionally motivated airmen.

Chapter 10

Deborah Leone Berg

Malcolm met his future wife Deborah Leone in 1972. Debbie and Malcolm both worked in the dental clinic in Wiesbaden Regional Medical Center where he was assigned as a dental technician. She was a work study student in the orthodontic clinic.

They worked together for about eight months before they started dating in 1973. When they met, Airman First Class Malcolm Berg was nineteen and Debbie was sixteen. They dated briefly from 1973 to 1974 and fell in love. The courtship was approved by her tight-knit, Italian-German family. They married in 1975. Malcolm and Debbie were compatible, having the same intellect, personality type, values, and religion. She was raised Catholic; he was Episcopalian—close enough. Both were from Air Force families.

Deborah's father, Frank P. Leone, was born in Middletown, Connecticut, on December 19, 1929. He graduated from Woodrow Wilson High School and immediately joined the Army Air Corps in 1948. Stationed in Germany, he married a German national in 1952. He spent over thirty years in printing and reproduction for the Air Force.

Frank Sr. was one of the top enlisted men in the Air Force as a chief master sergeant (E-9). Frank Sr. had a successful thirty-year career in the Air Force. He liked Malcolm and enthusiastically supported the budding relationship. Both Frank Sr. and Malcolm entered the U.S. Air Force from high school.

His son, Frank Jr., followed in his father's footsteps and enlisted in the US Air Force. He was an inflight refueling specialist. Frank Jr. married his wife Linda, a US Army medic.

As Malcolm's older brother, I was asked to be the best man at their wedding. Malcolm provided a detailed itinerary from the United States, including the airplane tickets and the currency for each of the countries I would cross. I traveled in the winter, flying from Illinois to Iceland to Luxemburg, then by train back through Belgium and part of France into Germany. It was stunning to look out of the speeding train's window as snow-covered Europe zipped by while listening to the relaxing clickety clack of the train's wheels.

The exact timing and schedule were well thought out and thorough. It was planned like an Air Force bombing mission—on time, on target. However, circumstances and the translation from American English to German confused the cab driver on the last leg of the journey. I was late. At the wedding ceremony, they waited as long as they could before caring on without me. The best man was tardy by a few hours.

The newlywed couple planned their honeymoon to ski in Germany and Austria, now with their best man in tow. We zipped down the autobahn (no speed limits) cramped together in their light blue Volkswagen, listening to the rock music of

10.1. Malcolm and Deborah Berg's wedding, 1975

the New Riders of The Purple Sage. We skied, laughed, and drank beer and peppermint schnaps all the way to and through the Alps.

We skied in Garmisch near the famous Zugspitze in the German Alps. The next and the most memorable ski area was in Kitzbuhel, in the Austrian Alps of Tirol. We conquered the famous (and most difficult) Hahnenkamm ski run in Austria with only minor injuries. We had fun, but I was never forgiven for being late for the wedding.

Malcolm was ambitious and, with a beautiful young wife, more than ever wanted to be successful. He decided not to reenlist in the Air Force when his four-year contract was complete. He was determined to attend college, with the goal of being accepted into dental school and returning to the Air Force as an officer. He was confident in his skills and his ability to learn and knew he would succeed.

Chapter 11

College in Illinois

WHEN HIS INITIAL ENLISTMENT was up, Malcolm returned to the States, applied to, and was accepted as an undergraduate at Southern Illinois University in Carbondale (SIU-C). Carbondale has one of the most beautiful college campuses in the Midwest. It's near the Shawnee National Forest, with easy access to the Little Grassy, Crab Orchard, and Devil's Kitchen lakes. SIU-C is at the southernmost end of the state, known for its fertile soil. The area was nicknamed Little Egypt because of it. The SIU-C mascot is the Saluki, an Egyptian sighthound. SIU-C was also voted as the number one party school in the United States by Playboy magazine in the late 1960s. "We didn't win many games, but we never lost a party. Ooh-poo-pah-doo SIU!"

Malcolm and Debbie enjoyed Carbondale and all the attractions and distractions while he finished his undergraduate degree. Malcolm used the GI bill to help support them, but they both worked. He was a janitor; she worked as an office receptionist. While at SIU-C, Debbie got her Bachelor of Science degree in dental hygiene.

They attended SIU-C from 1975 to 1978. Malcolm combined his University of Maryland extension coursework with his undergraduate studies and graduated with a Bachelor of Science degree in Biochemistry.

Malcolm applied to several dental schools and was accepted at each. The best choice was SIU in Edwardsville, Illinois. They were used to the Southern Illinois University system; they paid in-state tuition, and the school's reputation was good. After a brief reprieve and celebration with family, it was off to dental school!

There is nothing easy about dental school, even with four years of experience in clinics. There was only one year remaining on his GI bill, so loans and jobs were necessary. Malcolm's classmates asked for help with pharmacology, so he was employed by the school as a tutor. He also was elected president of his dental school class.

There were a few musicians in his dental school class, and they formed a group "The Ghost Riders," which lasted long after dental school. They played together in dive bars, weddings, school functions, and venues in the greater St. Louis area.

Malcolm and Debbie didn't hesitate when the Air Force offered him a direct commission as a captain and choice of duty station. After Malcolm completed a two-week officer training and orientation, Debbie pinned on his captain bars.

Another US Air Force journey had just begun.

It was easier for Malcolm as prior enlisted; the mysteries of military customs and courtesies were already familiar. Debbie was about to become an officer's wife, with implied new responsibilities for herself, her husband, and his direct reports, usually young airmen. With her experience as a military dependent, it was a natural transition; she was born into the job.

Chapter 12

Back to the Air Force

IN 1982, MALCOLM AND Debbie were assigned to the British Royal Air Force base at Lakenheath, England, as their first duty station. The base is the home of 48th Tactical Fighter Wing and the F-111 Aardvark Fighter Bomber.

They settled in quickly, making friends and traveling all over the island. Malcolm retraced some of his steps as a young lad, sightseeing many of the places he was told he had seen before.

The US Air Force encourages officers and enlisted airmen to continue their educations. Malcolm took advantage of the opportunity and received his master's degree in business

12.1. Captain M R Berg, Royal Air Base, Lakenheath, England, 1982

administration (MBA) with a concentration in management from the University of Maryland.

One of Malcolm's duties included assisting mortuary affairs with body identification using the deceased's dental record. Identification of remains is normally a function of the US Army Mortuary Affairs. However, Malcolm was trained in forensic dentistry in San Antonio and provided military and civilian body identification for plane crashes, automobile wrecks, and building fires.

Another aspect of the dental service is performing battle-casualty triage, involving prioritizing treatment of patients based on the severity of their wounds and injuries, then directing the patient to the appropriate surgeon or doctor. Captain Berg had a course in triage and also trained as an anesthesia extender while in England.

Additionally, military medical and dental personnel must be ready for the fight if needed. To prepare doctors, dentists, and advanced practice nurses, they undergo simulated combat training. The training usually includes setting up temporary field hospitals and emergency services, weapons training, and physical fitness.

Malcolm recalled that at Camp Bullis, outside San Antonio, the weeklong training included repelling from a thirty-foot training tower. The training was conducted by a lance corporal Marine (E-3). The young Marine asked all the officers if any of them were afraid of heights. Malcolm thought nothing of the question; it was easy to answer, so he raised his hand.

The enlisted Marine approached Malcolm and said, "Thank you, sir. You'll be first."

Malcolm rolled his eyes as he donned the leather gloves and climbed the wooden tower stairs. For the record, he said he did well and made it down safely.

While in England, their first son, a future US Air Force officer, was born. His name was Stephen Charles Berg.

TEXAS

Debbie's father, Frank Sr., a chief master sergeant with a stellar Air Force career behind him, retired in Texas. When it was time to rotate to a new duty station in 1986, Malcolm requested and got assigned to Bergstrom Air Force Base.

Bergstrom Air Force Base is located east of Austin, in Traverse County, Texas. Malcolm and Debbie enjoyed the close association with family. They also became dedicated fans of the University of Texas football Longhorns. With fellow rabid fans, they turned tailgating before and after Longhorn football games into a fashionable celebration of food and drink.

They got to know Texas well, enjoying the unique culture and blends of Mexican and American foods (TexMex). They learned to appreciate that chili either has meat and peppers or meat, peppers and beans, depending on how far south you travel. Smoked beef brisket and Shiner Bock beer were regular features while dining in or dining out.

Texans have pride in their state unrivaled by any other state, according to many natural-born Texans. While stationed at Bergstrom, their second son Michael Berg was born a pride-filled Texan.

Malcolm was promoted to the rank of major in 1988.

MISSOURI

In 1992, Malcolm was transferred to the dental clinic as part of the 509th Bomb Wing, Whiteman Air Force Base, Missouri. Whiteman is the home of the B-2 Spirit bomber one of the US Air Force's most lethal weapons. The base is a strategic keystone in projecting American power worldwide.

Whiteman is near the town of Knob Noster and about sixty miles south of Kansas City, Missouri. It was formerly Sedalia Army Airfield in WWII. There was a certain prestige serving at one of the most important bases in the US Air Force. While at Whiteman, Malcolm was promoted to lieutenant colonel.

The security surrounding the base and the arsenal of stealthy jets is layered, starting with the perimeter and even in the nearby community. Stationed at Whiteman, many Air Force families became close and socialized amongst themselves. Malcolm and Debbie developed close friendships that are long lasting.

But the couple loved Europe, and when the opportunity to serve in Germany was offered, they accepted.

GERMANY

In 1995, Lieutenant Colonel Berg and his four-part family packed up once again and headed to Germany. Ramstein Air Force Base was where Malcolm had spent time as a boy. It was his first choice for their next assignment. They were delighted to share Germany and Europe with their two young sons. Travel and sporting events were the center of their lives.

Comeback falls short

The Ramstein Senior All-stars baseball team dug themselves into a hole early and were never able to climb completely out as they took third in the European Regional Championships in Brzeg, Poland July 13 to 19.

Ramstein dropped their opener to Lithuania 5-2 and had to fight their way back through the losers bracket. There they registered successive victories over hosts Brzeg, Lithuania, in an emotional extra-inning rematch, and Russia.

Without any days off, the tired arms of the pitching staff finally gave out late in game five, and Ramstein was eliminated by Poland. Several individual performances made Ramstein the obvious crowd favorite. Aaron D'LaToille had four home runs, each well over 400 feet. Stephen Berg batted a tournament high .706, swatting five doubles in the process. Dan Thompson entertained the crowed with several running catches in center field, and had the defensive play of the tournament, throwing out a runner tagging from third base. Ramstein finished the post season with a 9-2 record.

12.2. Ramstein All Star baseball team in Poland. Steve batted a tournament-high .706, 1997

Stephen and Michael participated in almost every sport offered, and they excelled in all of them. The boys swam competitively, and their baseball teams won several European league championships.

But it was soccer (*Fussball* in German) where they placed most of their emphasis, sometimes with and sometimes against German teams. The boys had several European coaches who pushed them to play like Europeans. Malcolm and Debbie vocally coached from the bleachers and served as chauffeurs every step of the way.

When not at sports tournaments and games, traveling Europe was a priority. The Air Force family experienced much of what Europe offered: culture, language, history, and food. Driving to France for the afternoon was an easy day trip. On a lark, they flew to Turkey for Thanksgiving.

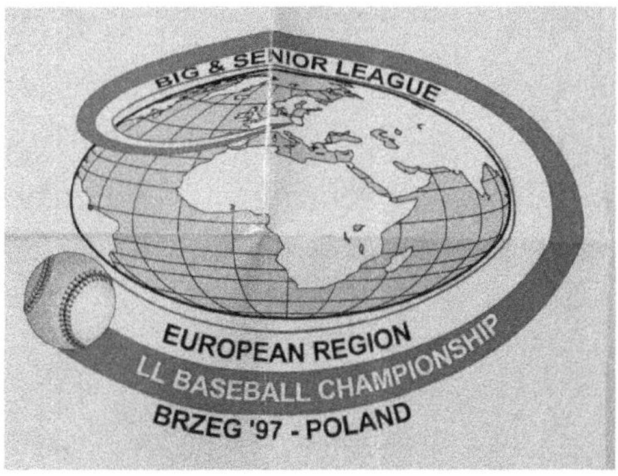

12.3. Ramstein Senior Little League in Poland, 1997

12.4. Turkey for Thanksgiving, 1997

Ramstein, although much different from Malcolm's first visit, was still a NATO base. It was common to interact with a variety of people. In 1998, their tour of duty came to an end with Malcolm retiring as a lieutenant colonel after twenty years of service, both as an enlisted airman and as an officer.

TEXAS

They were sad to leave Germany but happy they were headed once again to Austin, Texas. Malcolm and Debbie opened several private dental clinics, eventually totaling five offices in south central Texas.

In 2022, they retired to the Hill Country in south Texas. They spend time enjoying their retirement and the successes afforded by the US Air Force and their drive and ambition.

The family tradition of US Air Force service was handed off to Malcolm and Debbie's oldest son Stephen.

SECTION 4

Chapter 13

Stephen Charles Berg

Stephen Charles Berg was born on December 12, 1982, at RAF Lakenheath, England, where his father Malcolm was stationed.

Stephen was an easy child and always wanted to please his parents. He was well-behaved, intelligent, and athletic. He won countless youth swimming competitions in both Missouri and Europe. Stephen played in the Junior League World Series baseball tournament representing Germany when he was thirteen.

Texas

In Austin, Texas, Stephen attended Bowie High School and graduated in 2001. He was accepted into Texas Lutheran University (TLU) in Seguin, a small, private university noted for its preprofessional curriculums. Stephen played soccer and earned four varsity letters. He majored in biology and graduated cum laude in 2005.

After graduating from TLU, he worked in his parent's dental clinic until he was accepted to Nova Southeastern University, Fort Lauderdale, Florida, in 2011. Stephen studied for a master's degree in science and was accepted into the dental school, signing a contract with the US Air Force for a scholarship to help pay for the tuition.

In 2011, he met Molly Chesson through mutual friend in Fort Lauderdale. Molly had graduated from the University of North Carolina–Wilmington with a degree in business administration. They were married in Wimberley, Texas, on December 12, 2011. Stephen's younger brother Mike was the best man. The wedding celebration lasted into the night—Texas style. A highlight of the evening after party was Malcolm's guitar solo, playing a rousing rendition of Chuck Berry's song "Johnny B Goode."

ALABAMA

Soon after graduation from dental school, Stephen and Molly entered active duty in the United States Air Force Dental Corps. Stephen attended the Officer Training School (OTS) at Maxwell Air Force Base in Montgomery, Alabama, a five-week course for professionals who receive a direct commission. Typically, these officers have advanced graduate level degrees, often master's or doctorates. The professions include physicians and dentists among others. They enter as first lieutenant or captains, commensurate with their higher levels of education.

The officer training school is responsible for developing cadets into professional officers by instilling character, knowledge, and motivation essential to serving in the United States Air Force.

After an initial, shocking boot-camp experience, the first few weeks of training are geared toward the cadet becoming familiar with Air Force standards. The focus is on physical training, drilling, customs and courtesies, ceremonies, and academics. Cadets are expected to work for their fellow flight and squadron members to accomplish specific tasks as required by the flight commander and cadet wing.

Stephen attended multiple classes in an academic environment. Later in the program, he attended field training exercises, small arms training, and build team skills by overcoming challenges in a simulated deployment environment. To graduate, cadets must meet or exceed physical, academic, and military-bearing standards. Military bearing includes the ability to write and verbally express themselves professionally. Molly, Malcolm, Debbie, and I enjoyed the dignified graduation ceremony in Alabama.

NEBRASKA

After graduating from OTS, Stephen completed a one-year residency in advanced education in clinical dentistry in 2012 at Offutt, Air Force Base, located south of Omaha, Nebraska.

Omaha is the home of the US Strategic Command and hosts the 557th Weather Wing and the 55th Wing of Air Combat Command. Offutt is best known for having been the home of the centerpiece of American's air defense, the Strategic Air Command, until 1992.

Stephen and Molly lived off base in a comfortable apartment. Molly made friends with other young officers' wives and frequently entertained the couples at the officers' club on base. Molly received and gracefully accepted tips from Debbie Berg (her mother-in-law) about the challenges and opportunities of an Air Force officer's wife.

After completing the residency, Stephen and Moly were assigned to Kadena Air Force Base, Okinawa, Japan.

JAPAN

The family served at Kadena Air Force Base in Okinawa, Japan, from 2012 to 2015. Okinawa is the largest island in the Okinawan Island chain but the smallest of the five main Japanese Islands. It's approximately 400 miles south of the main island Kyushu and the rest of Japan.

The imperial Japanese surrendered in WWII on September 2, 1945, when the US gained control of the island and occupied it from 1945 until 1952. The US gradually returned control of the various islands, completing the transition in 1971. However, there remains more than two dozen US military bases on the island since 1951. US military bases account for 4-5 percent of the island economy. With 120 active military bases in Japan, 70 percent are in or around Okinawa.

On Okinawa, Stephen earned the United States Air Force Accommodation Medal and other group medals citations and awards for outstanding performance as a dentist and his other responsibilities in the clinic. While he was in Japan, he completed Squadron Officer School.

Brynley, their first daughter, was born June 17, 2014, in the US Marine Corps base hospital at Camp Foster in Ginowan, Okinawa, Japan, the largest naval hospital outside of the continental US.

While enjoying a new daughter and family life, Stephen was on the fast track in the Air Force. Given the opportunity to someday return, they agreed to accept another Japan assignment if one was offered.

In the meantime, they were relocated to Texas in 2015.

TEXAS

Completing their tour of duty in Okinawa, Stephen was selected for a two-year residency in comprehensive dentistry at Lackland Air Force Base, in San Antonio, Texas.

Their second daughter Adelyn (Addy) was born on March 25, 2016, at the combined-service medical complex known as Brooke Army Medical Center. The hospital is located at the Joint Base San Antonio–Fort Sam Houston, which hosts the Academy of Health Sciences, educating military medical personnel from all branches of the service.

The residency training was intense and challenging but helped cement his career as an Air Force dentist. Captain Berg was awarded the very competitive and coveted "Best Resident Research Project" and promoted to the rank of major.

JAPAN

As a new major, Stephen requested and was granted a second duty in Japan in 2017. He served four years at Yokota Air Force Base near Tokyo, headquarters for the US Forces Japan and the Fifth Air Force. It's also the headquarters of the Japanese Self Defense Force (JSDF) Air Defense Command. The base functions as a strategic airlift hub and is the home of the 374th Airlift Wing and the 515th Air Mobility Group.

The base is situated on the Kanto Plain about twenty-eight miles northwest of Tokyo, within the political boundaries of six municipalities in the Tokyo prefecture. The area immediately surrounding the base is the city of Fussa. Originally it was opened in 1940 as Tama Army Airfield by the Imperial Japanese Army. The base was renamed Yokota Air Base in 1946.

While stationed at Yokota, Stephen was appointed as chief of general dentistry. Based on his residency, he was recognized as expert in his field.

Based on his research, Major Berg was invited to provide general dentistry lectures in China, Tokyo, and Guam. He was honored to present his western dental knowledge in China. When he returned, he described the experience as "educational," saying that the Chinese were sensitive and secretive. They restricted outside communication and limited cell phone access. Cell phones had to be surrendered when they entered the country. Stephen also said his Chinese hosts were slightly arrogant and dismissive of the invited American medical and dental contingent.

Back in Japan, Stephen enjoyed being responsible for his duties in the clinic. He was awarded the Air Force Meritorious

Service Medal for his efforts in keeping the Yokota Air Force Base Dental Clinic virtually free of COVID-19 cases, the only clinic in the Air Force to do so.

In the meantime, both daughters attended the international school with Japanese children and other American service member dependents. The school was a highly enriched educational environment. Brynley played soccer, enjoyed swimming competitively, and learned violin and piano. Addy was interested in dance, which developed into a love for gymnastics. Both spoke playground Japanese.

Stephen completed the Air Command and Staff College and served on a medical mission to Bangladesh. He reported that the two-week mission was in an austere environment and conditions were "rough." He felt sadden by the plight of the people in Bangladesh but was glad when the humanitarian mission was completed.

Upon his return, he was awarded the Meritorious Service Medal.

OKLAHOMA

Since 2021, Stephen has been serving as the dental service flight leader at Tinker Air Force Base in Oklahoma. In 2023-2024, he commanded dental teams from across the Air Force in various field exercises in Illinois and Tennessee, preparing troops for overseas deployments. Stephen was awarded a second United States Air Force Commendation Medal. He is currently (2025) enrolled in the Air War College at Tinker AFB.

Molly continues her studies toward her PhD in occupational therapy at the University of Oklahoma in Oklahoma City and will graduate in 2026. Brynley continues with her busy schedule playing piano and violin along with soccer and swimming. Adelyn continues with gymnastics and has her eye on cheerleading.

Stephen and Molly are carrying on the fourth generation— more than one hundred years of service in the US Air Force that began in 1917 with Herbert Parker and continued with Charles and Caroline Berg, Malcolm and Debbie Berg, and now Stephen and Molly Berg.

Maybe there will be a fifth generation.

SECTION 5

Chapter 14

What I Learned

I WAS CURIOUS ABOUT my grandfather and what he did in WWI. It was a curiosity I harbored for decades. As I researched his life, he became a different man than I had conjured up as a boy who spent summer vacations on the farm. Herbert became fun, clever, resourceful, and immensely strong after I realized the challenges he was faced with. He wasn't a patrician, spoiled, rich kid anymore. He worked hard and was dedicated to his farm and agriculture.

As I discovered more about him, I saw in my mind's eye the coy smile he used to give me when he discovered some devilish antic or dumb mistake I committed. I knew he liked me a lot by that subtle smile.

I learned the significant role my grandmother played in our lives. She seemed to appear out of nowhere wherever we were stationed. Researching the family, I was reminded how she managed the farm while Herbert was recovering from his injuries. When the harvesters came to the farm to bring in the oats, soybeans, or corn, she fed them breakfast, lunch, and dinner for her entire life. Joy was the center pillar of the family. She subtly kept everyone in line and balanced the conflicting demands of the extended family. Joy's roots were the hard scabble farming in North Dakota. She knew all the blackberry brambles on every dusty gravel country road in Lee

County, Illinois. Picking berries with her was not recreational, it was work. Riding in the family Buick a tornado was headed for grama and me, so we hurriedly bailed out of the car into a roadside ditch. In our haste we forgot the buckets of berries in the car. Joy got up and calmly walked to the car, rescued the berries and walked back to the ditch. The buckets were now safe, she slowly laid face down in the grass and smiled.

My grandfather Herbert Parker was a bomber pilot and gunner—not a fighter pilot like I was told. He enjoyed his family, particularly his sons, George and Gordon, and loved our mother, Caroline. I got to understand the difficulties of leaving the United States and flying in an experimental aircraft to a war that most men his age knew nothing about. Flying those early aircraft must have been cold, windy, uncomfortable, and extraordinarily dangerous.

I always had a great deal of respect for my grandfather and am now impressed with him as a younger man. He was no longer just a grandfather; I can see him as a dashing, young, bomber pilot in the World War.

My father, Charles, was adventurous, intelligent, and funny. He was clever and astute. Dad enjoyed his military experience. But most of all, the notion that he dearly loved our mother was reinforced.

His military career had its difficulties and disappointments. He withstood family rancor and slights with a shrug and a smile. He wasn't cut out to be an aircrew member, but he was perfectly suited for his roles in administration, recruiting, and public information. Dad stayed in the Air Force twenty-six years and would do anything for his family. He truly adored Elizabeth, our sister, and had a special affection for Malcolm.

I believe we had two separate periods in our family: one when Charles was in the Air Force and one when he retired to spend time with the family. He spent hours with both his younger children, playing whatever games Malcolm and Elizabeth enjoyed.

After his military retirement, Charles worked at a state institution for developmentally challenged boys and men. Every one of his coworkers said that he was a pleasure to work with. However, I think he longed for Jacksonville and his time on the St. Johns River.

When Dad passed away, he asked that his ashes be interned there. If he had to do it over, I believe that Dad would have lived in Florida or England for the rest of his life. Along with his southern attitudes, he was a committed Anglophile. He loved everything about England and the British. He stayed with this unique duality all his life—the fog of London or the fresh salt air of Florida.

By researching our Air Force story, I came to understand how intelligent, resourceful, and talented my brother Malcolm is. When he was serving in the Air Force, I had already graduated from high school and left home to serve in the Marines. Then I was off working in Colorado and California, enjoying my life as he continued his military career. Malcolm was more accomplished in everything he tried than I had believed.

He overcame many obstacles and hardships to get where he wanted to go, and I didn't give him the credit that was probably due. Older brothers are like that; we don't seem to give validity to our younger brothers. They are forever the little brother, even when they're adults.

In recent conversations with him, one thing stood out: Malcolm's respect for me because I never picked on him.

Like any good father, he wanted his sons to surpass his own achievements, and he played a part in making it happen through mentorship. Malcolm wanted his sons in military rank, education, and social standing to be better than his.

I enjoyed hearing from Malcolm about his son Stephen and his wife Molly. Stephen is so accomplished. He's been awarded many collegiate honors and Air Force medals. Because of the Air Force, Stephen and Molly have provided their daughters with an extraordinary early childhood and set the stage for their continued success.

I learned a lot about my Air Force family that I had not previously known. Now, they aren't just relatives; I see them as people with their strengths, and they're not-so-strong characteristics. In writing this book, I learned to love them even more.

There were triumphs and disappointments during the 100 years spanning the family's service in the United States Air Force. As a family traveling with the Air Force, we gained insight into others by experiencing a wide variety of cultures. Everyone enjoyed learning languages other than English, trying food, and listening to music and histories of other countries. Some of us tried pronouncing English with the local accents and with their area vernacular. It wasn't mockery; it was complimentary mimicry. I personally developed a slight Georgia slow-drawl accent when I felt like it. I liked the way it sounded.

We made friends; we lost friends. We felt the joy of meeting new people, and the pain of having to say goodbye, knowing we would probably not retrace the same steps ever again. Traveling to a new Air Force base, previous mistakes were erased, and we got to start fresh. Past personal victories were of no value to anyone except us; no one cared about what you did or where you used to live. As Air Force children, we had to re-establish ourselves with each new neighborhood or school. Being smart, clever, and funny helped. The boxing lessons didn't hurt either.

As children of the Air Force, we were all educated in different schools, by a variety of teachers. We learned self-discipline directly and vicariously, being exposed to the Air Force culture. For example, when a bugle sounded retreat (To the Colors) on a base or post, every truck, car, or bike, everybody and everything stopped what they were doing and faced the direction of the American flag. As little boys, we stood rigid at the position of attention. The short pause was more than a custom signaling the end of the workday. The evening ritual instilled respect in us and our families for America. Standing quietly for the lowering of the America flag was an honor and demonstrated respect rarely found outside the military.

We traveled a lot as many Air Force families tend to do. We were privileged to see much of the world. We experienced our fair share of inconsistency and push-pull in our lives, but with few exceptions, we all enjoyed our Air Force experiences and living in different places. Relocating to a new duty station gave us the sense that nothing was ever over. We led temporary lives.

Our experiences, friends, games, childhoods, and careers were constantly expanding. Everything was fresh and new. However, conclusions were hard to come by. Our lives were built in layers—one lamination on another. We gained strengths and weaknesses as a result, in different places in different ways. The US Air Force expanded our horizons and enlarged our world.

The Air Force shaped our family. In some important ways, our more than 100 hundred years of family service and families like ours helped shape the US Air Force.

We are blessed to be a United States Air Force family.

Acknowledgement

A SPECIAL THANK YOU to Major Alex Beckstrand, USMCR, PhD, and Legacies of Service for the detailed research on 2Lt Herbert N Parker and WWI.

Malcolm, Debbie, Stephen, and Molly Berg. Elizabeth (Berg) Nagy, photographs and personal recollections.

Notes

CHAPTER 2

The Lee County Genealogical and Historical Society (LCGHS)wrote a review of the inlet swamp.

In place of the water in which grew gigantic rushes, Indian rice and other worthless vegetation the home of millions of geese, ducks, swan, pheasant, grouse, wild Turkey, and other wild game. There came in gradual growth of course slew grass some short and mingled with weeds in great variety other kinds of rank and tall growing to heights of 10 or 12 feet. The land was overflowed during the spring and early summer but later unless the season was wet the water dried off and the sod which was of very tough nature could bear up a team and loaded wagon during the fall of the year. After the grass had been killed by frost's magnificence. Prairie fires prevailed until snow came. The flames at night when there were high winds lighting up the sky with surprising grandeur enabling a person to read by the light miles away and being visible for 100 miles.

The swamp was created by a solid rock formation a thick ledge that prevented the enormous, primordial swamp from draining. Water was backed up for miles by the ancient stone barrier. Various attempts were made to cut through the rock, but the cost was prohibitive. Local farmers grazed cattle and horses around the swamp as foraging cost nothing.

From time to time, committees were formed to develop the swamplands. A few people recognized the potential value of the land and suggested a variety of uses including creating a mill for processing grains.

When one portion of the natural rock dam was removed, the water level of 30,000 acres was lowered. Farmers used the now-drier land as a herding ground. It was open range for cattle and horses with few, if any, fences.

Over time the wild grass improved in quality. At first it cost nothing but the labor of cutting, curing, and hauling, but in a few years, its value became known to the mostly absentee landowners, and hay sold for $0.50 to $1.50 an acre standing. During the extremely dry summer of 1887, the farmers and liveryman coming from Polo and Oregon and even farther bought the standing hay for $1.00 to $1.50 an acre (LCGHS).

Around 1837, attracted by reports of the beauty of the Rock River and the area surrounding it, people of "cultivated tastes and refinement with considerable property closed out their holdings in the eastern States and migrated to the area around Dixon" (LCGHS).

The land all around the swamp was becoming more valuable and that attracted a great deal of interest. Wealthy eastern investors wanted to incorporate the land for hunting clubs or farms. Some investors were land speculators, counting on the soil revealed by partially draining the swamp to be a mineral rich, extraordinarily fertile, black loam.

To increase the drainage—thus increasing the value of its surrounding land—a cut of the inlet rock barrier was made twenty feet wider, down to within a few feet of the bottom. In 1895, few visionaries residing in the central part of the state understood the worth of the project.

The LCGHS made mention of Herbert's grandfather's contribution to the rise in value of the property.

With the rest of the lands of the district, these non-resident landowners were represented by Mr. E.F. Nichols of Delavan,

Illinois whose intelligent judgement and persistent laborers in supporting the commissioners promoting the interests of the district's deserves to be here recognized as well-nigh invaluable.

CHAPTER 4

The rise of a militaristic Germany and the decline of the Ottoman Empire disturbed the long-standing balance of power in Europe. Imperial rivalries, shifting alliances, and an arms and navy race between the great powers exacerbated the already tenuous situation in Europe.

Growing tensions between the great powers reached a breaking point on June 28, 1914, when a Bosnian Serb assassinated the heir to the Austro-Hungarian throne. Austria-Hungary blamed Serbia and declared war. Russia mobilized its Serbian defense, and Germany declared war on Russia and France, who had an alliance.

More than one author I consulted indicated that England participated in a variety of ways to accelerate the start of the war. The primary reason was the fear of the growing German navy and its potential to displace "Britannia rules the waves" as the anthem goes. The book *Pity the War* by Niall Ferguson provided us with the most detailed and plausible reason to doubt the conventional and widely accepted cause of WWI.

The United Kingdom declared war after Germany invaded Belgium. The Ottomans joined the Central Powers in November. The German strategy in 1914 was to quickly defeat France then transfer its forces to the east. However, its advances were halt in September, and by the end of the year, the Western Front consisted of a near-continuous line of trenches from the English Channel to Switzerland. The eastern front was more dynamic, but neither side gained a decisive advantage despite costly offenses. Italy, Bulgaria, Romania, Greece, and others entered the war in 1915 and onward.

The United States, after much resistance, entered the WWI on April 6, 1917. There were a variety of reasons the United States entered the war in Europe. The primary cause was unrestricted submarine warfare and the sinking of four American merchant ships. At that time there was also a growing alliance between Germany and Mexico. That inflamed public opinion and gradually changed how American citizens regarded entering a war in Europe.

Various sources describe the situation with Mexico and the proposed alliance with Germany each with its own perspective. Mexico was officially neutral in WWI but became a hidden theater of diplomatic and economic (spying). The 1917 Zimmermann Telegram was a secret German message sent from the German Foreign Secretary to Mexico, proposing an alliance against the US in exchange for the return of lost territories of the southwestern states (Arizona, Texas, and New Mexico). However, the complex relationships with the US and European powers—namely Britain who bought most of their oil products from Mexico—discouraged our southern neighbor from becoming a full-fledged participant in the war.

In addition, the Mexican Revolution was in full swing during WWI. The country was too preoccupied with its own civil war to become a major participant in a global conflict. However, German agents (spies and saboteurs) were in Mexico, including one who claimed responsibility for a munitions explosion in California and may have been involved in a 1916 explosion in New Jersey.

Germany had businesses in Mexico under heavy British and US surveillance.

One of the first uses of airplanes in combat by America was in 1916 by General John J. "Blackjack" Pershing. The Curtiss JNs are the same airplanes Herbert learned to fly. Pershing used the newly designed Curtiss JN as reconnaissance aircraft.

Pershing led an expedition into northern Mexico to hunt down revolutionary leader Pancho Villa who had raided a US town in New Mexico. The over-the-border incursion by Villa was to force repayment for faulty weapons he bought from American gun runners. When the sellers refused to make repayment, the popular version was that Villa shot them.

Initially public opinion was neutral or against a war in Europe. Americans were overwhelmingly isolationists. The United States had strong financial ties to countries in Europe, so what happened in that theater of operation affected the US, whether the citizens wanted to believe it or not. Scaremongering and government propaganda portrayed Germany as an aggressor threatening America.

Not everyone was keen on joining in on the war. Approximately 30,000 American draft evaders called "slackers" (about 10 percent of American draft-eligible men) took shelter and sought protection in Mexico.

Chapter 5

By September 1918 when Second Lieutenant Parker arrived in France, the American Expeditionary Force had finally established an independent American Army to fight alongside the British and French on the Western Front. In mid-September, they attacked the Saint Mihiel salient bulge in the allied lines. This test was important in preparation for the Allied offensive to launch their counterattack later in the month. For the Americans, this larger operation was known as Meuse-Argonne Offensive and lasted until signing of the Armistice in November.

Chapter 6

The job of a tail gunner was particularly dangerous due to its exposed position. Casualty reports indicate 17 percent killed and 12 percent wounded rate for B17 tail gunners in the Eighth Air Force in Europe. The tail gunners were positioned in the very rear of the B17. It was the prime target for enemy aircraft and anti-aircraft artillery.

Crewmembers also faced extremely cold temperatures and slipstream from the aircraft speed. The gunner had to deal with spent shell casings piling up around his feet, making the task even more uncomfortable. Only 36 percent of bomber crewmembers made it through their required tours of twenty-five missions.

CHAPTER 12

Bergstrom Air Force Base was activated on September 19, 1942, as Del Valle Army Air Base, constructed on 3,000 acres leased from the city of Austin. The name of the base was changed to Bergstrom Army Airfield on March 3, 1943, in honor of Captain John A.E. Bergstrom who was killed at Clark Field, Philippine Islands, on December 8, 1941. He was the first Austenite killed in World War II. The base was renamed Bergstrom Field November 11, 1943, and became Bergstrom Air Force Base in December 1948.

Initially Bergstrom was the home of the troop-carrying units. The base was at various times assigned to the Strategic Air Command and the Tactical Air Command. After July 1966, it was under the control of Tactical Air Command and was the headquarters of the 12th Air Force, which was responsible for all tactical air command reconnaissance, fighter, and airlift operations west of the Mississippi River.

On September 30, 1993, Bergstrom was officially closed and eventually became Austin airport (paraphrased from the Texas State Historical Association–Art Leatherwood).

References

Air Force Historical Research Agency. U.S. Air Force. Various records.

American Heroes Who Flew for France in World War I. New York: Atlantic Monthly Press, 2015.

Ancestry.com. Genealogical database. Accessed via Ancestry.com.

Army Morning Reports, World War II era. Accessed via Fold3.

Cameron, Rebecca Hancock. *Training to Fly: Military Flight Training*, 1907–1945.

Canadian Over-Seas Expeditionary Force. Attestation Paper, December 28, 1915.

Castelano, Ellen. *History UK: The History and Heritage Accommodation Guide.*

Center of Military History, United States Army. Unit history records.

Clifford, John Gary. *The Citizen Soldiers: The Plattsburg Training Camp Movement, 1913–1920.* Lexington: University Press of Kentucky, 1972.

Department of the Air Force. Military Personnel Records Division.

Fold3. Military records database.

Ferguson, Niall. *The Pity of War.* New York: Penguin Books, 1999.

Flood, Charles Bracelen. *First to Fly: The Story of the Lafayette Escadrille.*

Hynes, Samuel. *The Unsubstantial Air: American Fliers in the First World War.* New York: Farrar, Straus and Giroux, 2014.

Illinois Secretary of State Archives. Illinois State World War I Bonus Records.

Lee County Historical and Genealogical Society. Dixon, IL.

Luebke, Frederick. *Bonds of Loyalty: German-Americans and World War I.*

National Archives and Records Administration. World War I Strength Returns. Record Group 407. College Park, MD.

National Personnel Records Center. St. Louis, MO.

National Rifle Association. *American Rifleman.*

Phi Delta Theta Foundation. Letter (email), December 28, 2009. Oxford, OH.

Texas State Historical Association. Leatherwood, Art.

University of Wisconsin. *Directory of Officers and Students, 1916–1917.*

University of Wisconsin. Recommendation for Admission from Accredited School, July 21, 1916.

White, Gary. *The Great War Society: Relevance Archive.* Ellington Field History—First Formation Flight, 1918.

Other references are noted in the text.

About the Author

GEORGE HAS AN AAS degree from Sauk Valley College and a BS from Colorado State University. He is the retired president of Construction Research, Inc. George has published a wide variety of articles in industry journals and trade magazines.

He served in the United States Marine Corps as an infantry rifleman fire team leader. George was awarded two Purple Hearts, the Presidential Unit Citation, Navy Marine Corps Combat Action Badge, and the National Defense Service Medal, among others.

9 798995 280101